D1128491

Custom Tailoring

for Homemakers

Custom Tailoring
for Homemakers

Doris May Beck
Teacher, Custom Tailoring
St. Louis Board of Education

Drawings by **Ruth Hoessle Freeman**

Chas. A. Bennett Co., Peoria, Illinois

Copyright 1964

By DORIS MAY BECK

All rights reserved

Library of Cong. Cat. No. 64-14339

PRINTED IN THE UNITED STATES OF AMERICA
Third Printing
36VH610

DEDICATION

To my friends and students, whose encouragement inspired the
writing of this book on the fine art of tailoring

Contents

Preface

To take a beautiful piece of material and create a garment is as much an art as to take a palette and brush and create a painting. Like painting, tailoring requires a skill which can be gained by anyone who has a real interest in creating beautiful clothes.

The information in this book, gleaned from years of research and teaching experience in the field of tailoring, has been simplified. The instructions are presented in a descriptive and illustrative manner and, if they are followed, the art of tailoring can be mastered. This book encompasses basic techniques and finer points of tailoring that are necessary to produce a well-tailored garment.

The author wishes to express her appreciation to Ruth Freeman, co-editor, for her illustrations and assistance, and to her daughters, Betty Jacobson and Norma Maxwell, for correcting and typing the manuscript.

1. Fabrics

Wool Most Important

Woolen fabric is the aristocrat of all materials. It is woven into summer and winter cloth. There are many styles and qualities of woolens to choose from today, and many factors in grading wool—where the animal lives, the part of the body from which the wool comes, and the kind of sheep or breed of animal sheared. Fabric designers have given us practical as well as glamorous woolens to assist the buyer in the final selection.

The market has several million sheep for the production of wool, but there is not enough wool to supply the world population. Therefore it is necessary to combine other fibers with wool to extend the supply: vicuna, llama, camel hair, goat hair, vegetable fibers, and synthetics. Typical part-wool fabrics are: wool and silk, wool and cotton, wool and rayon, wool and nylon (or its derivatives), and combinations including other synthetics such as Dacron or Acrilan. However, pure wool is still the most prized of all the fabrics.

Virgin wool is the first wool from the sheep. *Pulled* or *reclaimed* wool is reprocessed and used a second time.

It is said the Merino sheep has the finest and softest wool, which therefore is graded very highly. Wool is produced in many geographical locations, but Australia is first as the producer of the finest wool.

QUESTIONS

1. Why is wool the most important of all fabrics?
2. Describe and explain the differences between virgin wool, pulled wool, reclaimed wool, and combinations.
3. How is wool graded?

Weaving

The history of weaving is quite long and intriguing. Although it is not the purpose of this book to become involved in the detailed evolution of fabric weaving, you should pursue this subject in order to have a more comprehensive understanding of the fabrics used in tailoring. The primary concern of this section is with the main fabrics recommended for tailoring purposes.

Processing of Wool

Sheep wool, when skillfully sheared, clings together. It is easily bound in bales and sorted according to length of fiber. The fibers contain grease which must be boiled from the wool. This grease, called *yolk*, keeps the wool from matting, yet sheep get

9

extremely dirty because of their oily fleece.

After the bales are graded and boiled, they must be washed in warm, soapy water until the wool is white and clean; this is called *scouring*. It is then dried and sprayed with oil unless it has been stock dyed (while still wet).

Stock dyeing is most desirable because the wool fibers absorb the dye uniformly, resist fading, rubbing off, and color change from wear. The ancient expression "dyed in the wool" originated from this dyeing process.

Yarn dyeing usually produces deeper and richer color tones, and is necessary for fabrics with woven patterns, plaids, or stripes.

Piece dyeing is done after the fabric is woven. Fabric dyed by this method is not uniform in color and is usually less expensive than stock- or yarn-dyed fabrics.

QUESTIONS

1. Describe the processes involved from the shearing of sheep to spinning of the yarn.
2. What is yolk?
3. Explain the terms: stock-dyed, yarn-dyed, and piece-dyed. Which method is preferred?

Types of Manufactured Wool

There are two types of yarns, *worsteds* and *soft woolens*. Soft woolens, made of short, staple yarn with slack twist, weave into a soft, bulky fabric, weaker than worsted. Worsteds are made of long staple, tightly twisted, finer fibers, woven and singed to form hard, strong fabric.

Worsteds

Carding is the first step in making worsted fibers. The fibers are passed between rollers rotating in opposite directions. The rollers are equipped with small wire teeth, creating a combing action which separates and straightens the fibers into threads. These threads are picked up by a comb and wound into a ball.

Gilling, the straightening of fibers, is the next process. Short fibers are removed, as only long ones are used for worsted woolens. Gilling is repeated several times, then the fibers are wound on a finished spool. If the wool is not dyed while wet, it is dyed after scouring, either in the skein or ball, or after it is woven into yardage.

Roving, or *drawing*, means working with yarn until the proper size of thread is attained — single, double, triple, or quadruple strand — before winding on spools for weaving. The thread is now inspected for imperfections.

Two threads are used in weaving: the *warp thread* runs lengthwise in the material, and the *weft*, or *woof*, thread runs crosswise. The warp thread is stronger; that is why we cut reinforcement threads on warp, or lengthwise grain, of material.

After the material is woven into lengths it goes through a *burling* or *mending* process. At this point, a second scouring is necessary to remove the remaining oil and dirt.

Fulling is a process in which the cloth is run through a heavy roller, under great pressure, moistened with special soap. Now the wool is permanently dyed, rinsed, and dried.

Finally, it is run through a roller that brushes the long nap up and shears the fibers short. Here it receives its final inspection for flaws. When flaws are corrected, the wool is ready for the market. Woolens at this stage have not been fully shrunk.

After reading this brief summary, you can readily understand why worsted woolens make durable and expensive fabrics. The following are some *worsted trade names* that will enable you to distinguish between woolens and worsteds: Cheviot, covert, flannel, gabardine, serge, nun's veiling, challis, crepe, poiret twill, and whip cord. There are other types of worsteds, but these are more common.

Woolens

The process of carding and burling woolens is much the same as for worsteds, but the fibers do not have to be separated, combed, and gilled as much because they are shorter. The finishing of woolens varies, depending on whether or not they are dyed before scouring and fulling.

Face cloth or *broadcloth* is one of the finer woolens. The finishing of this type of material rather than the weaving increases its cost. It is run through a roller machine with lawn-mower-type shears, then steamed and brushed until the desired luster appears.

The more common woolens are coatings, chinchilla, duvetyns, tweeds, wool jersey, cashmere, homespun, beaver, broadcloth, and many more. The difference between worsteds and woolens is that woolens are soft and worsteds are hard-surfaced fabrics. Woolens are usually more dull in color than worsteds because of the looser, soft weave.

Reclaimed Wools

Reclaimed wool is a combination of virgin and old wool; it wears very well and the law requires thorough sterilization before weaving. Do not hesitate to use it on this account.

It is almost impossible to weave reclaimed wool into worsteds because of the short nap that affects carding the old material.

Pulled Wool

This is wool removed from the sheep after it is dead rather than shorn from the live animal, and is inferior in quality.

Blended Silk, Cotton, Rayon, and Wool

Wool fibers dye better than any other fibers and for this reason extreme care should be used when purchasing wool blends, because the colors may fade after a few wearings.

When buying a blended fabric, try to choose a color suitable for your climate. For instance, do not buy material that will sunstreak after a few weeks if you live where the climate is warm all year. Be careful when buying combined cottons, linens, and woolens, unless the percentage of wool is high. Also, because shrinkage is greater in wool than in other fibers, combined material can have a crinkled or wavy effect. Always check the label for the percentage of each fiber. This will enable you to use good judgment in selecting your fabric.

Beware of bargains when buying blended fabrics—what may seem to be a bargain may have inferior quality. Remember, lightweight woolens are better adapted for dresses, suits, and lighter-weight outer garments. Heavier woolens are used for coats, suit toppers, and winter suits.

QUESTIONS

1. How are wool fibers straightened?
2. Identify the two threads used in weaving piece material. Which runs parallel to the selvedge?
3. What effect does the fulling process have on fabric?
4. Name some worsted trade names.
5. Describe the differences in the processing of worsteds and woolens.
6. Why is broadcloth considered one of the finest woolen fabrics?
7. Name some woolen trade names.
8. What is meant by reclaimed wool? Is it safe to use?
9. Can reclaimed wool be woven into worsted fabric?
10. Why should caution be used in buying blended fabrics?

Testing Wool and Wool Combinations

Several methods for testing may be used in the classroom: Boil a small piece of wool-and-cotton cloth in 1 cup of water and 1 tablespoon of lye for 15 minutes. Rinse and run the cloth between the fingers. The wool will dissolve, leaving only the cotton fibers. When testing all white material, cover with 50 per cent nitric solution. The wool will become yellow, while the cotton stays white. Rinse in ammonia and the wool will turn orange.

Testing Wool-Silk

Place a piece of wool-silk material in hydrochloric acid for 3 or 4 minutes. The silk will dissolve, leaving the wool unaffected.

Testing Wool

The best test of wool is to burn the edge of a swatch of woolen material. True wool does not burn easily, nor make a large flame. It smolders and has the odor of burning hair and meat.

Some people rub the material across their tongue to taste it; they claim wool has an oily taste. This would take a real expert.

The best method for the inexperienced shopper is to buy from reliable dealers, and to depend on quality merchandise with renowned brand names.

There are many methods of testing woolens, but these are the most common.

QUESTION

1. How do you test wool, wool and cotton, wool and silk?

Lining Materials

Pure silk was formerly a luxury, enjoyed only by the wealthy. Today, science has cultivated silkworm farms that aid in producing a plentiful supply for silk factories, and the economy-conscious woman can select pure silk for her wardrobe because it is practical as well as elegant.

Silk crepe, tissue faille, satin, and satin-back crepe are recommended for suit and coat linings because they are more durable than the soft, shimmering silk fabrics. Satin, rayon, and celanese rayon makes satisfactory linings, although they do not have the wearability of silk and crepe. A good lining material for summer garments is silk bemberg, or lightweight rayon-crepe.

All types of lining materials can be tailored according to the instructions in this book. However, the inexperienced student should use care in choosing lining fabric for a garment— silk with silk and cotton with cotton.

QUESTION

1. What fabrics are most suitable for linings and what factors guide this choice?

Choosing Fabrics

People may choose material just because it has eye-appeal. Visual selection alone is not recommended for the inexperienced because there are many other factors to consider.

1. Is the material practical for your mode of living? For instance, a silk brocade suit is impractical for business or sportswear.

2. Is the color attractive on you, or did you buy it because it looked pretty on the bolt? For example, a titian haired lass should never choose red. Also, consider the color of your accessories before you select a fabric.

3. What type of material should you purchase? Carefully select your material to make certain the design and texture will compliment your figure. The large figure looks best with smooth dark shades, simple in design; the petite figure (5 feet and under) should avoid nubby or bulky fabrics, although the choice is greater than for the larger figure; and the tall, slender figure goes with any standard fabric. The size of the individual should be considered when choosing plaids or patterned fabrics. The petite figure should avoid large plaids because they "weigh" one down. Leave the large plaids and design patterns for the tall, slender, or medium-tall figure. Always drape the material over the body, in front of a mirror, before

making a purchase. Plan carefully before you choose fabric and pattern.

4. What does your budget permit you to spend? If your budget is limited, buy the best and the most conservative fabric you can afford. Each year change your color, or accessories, to enlarge your wardrobe. Well-tailored clothes, expertly fitted in your most becoming style, will last many seasons before they appear outmoded.

If you see a beautiful garment on display and cannot afford to buy it, you can recreate the garment by drafting a pattern. Some tailoring concerns will draft patterns for a nominal fee. If you are unable to duplicate the fabric of the original design, select a related material. There is greater charm in adapting an original than in commercial patterns and ready-made garments. Strive for individuality in design and workmanship. These accomplishments impart personal satisfaction, make you "individual." Clothes should reflect your personality, bring out your best character traits and physical features.

QUESTIONS

1. What four factors do you consider in choosing fabrics?
2. What can you do to give originality to your clothes?

2. Basic Techniques

Necessary Equipment

1. Large cutting table or floor space.

2. Sharp cutting shears at least 8″ long, and small, sharp scissors, about 6″ in length, for snipping threads, cutting buttonholes, and snipping seams.

3. Tailor's chalk (clay preferred).

4. Non-stretch tape measure, 12″ ruler with markings from 1/16″ to 1″, and a yardstick. A curved tailor's ruler if you draw your own patterns.

5. Two sizes of needles: No. 8 in-betweens for finishing, and No. 5 for basting and pad sewing.

6. Sharp dressmaker pins. A pin cushion.

7. Open-end tailor's thimble because:

• You can wear it constantly while working.

• You can train yourself to work from the side of the finger instead of the end, thus leaving your wrist more relaxed and the tip of your finger free to handle material more easily.

8. A sewing machine that will make heavy seams.

9. Ironing board, chemical press cloth, and wool press cloth. Block of hardwood for pounding seams. Edge board, or seam board, and sleeve board are helpful, but the small end of the ironing board may be substi-

tuted for shrinking fullness from sleeves.

10. Sponge and shallow pan for dampening press cloth.

11. Tailor's ham for pressing curves and darts. See instructions for making a tailor's ham.

12. Piece of beeswax.

13. A full length mirror for draping and trying on garments during construction.

14. A comfortable chair. Greater concentration may be achieved when the body is relaxed.

15. Various sizes of sandbags for pattern weights.

How to Make a Tailor's Ham

Tailor's hams are valuable in pressing shoulder darts, shaping busts, collars, lapels, or seams that curve over the body—skirt closures, darts, etc. When shrinking fullness from lapels, always use the tailor's ham, moving the iron with horizontal strokes toward the bust line. Molding a garment to fit the curves of the body is the secret of fine tailoring.

Cut two oval pieces of canvas, or heavy muslin, according to measurements, Fig. 1, page 16. Join together, leaving about 5″ open on the side for stuffing.

Trim seams, turn inside out, and fill with small pieces of wool material,

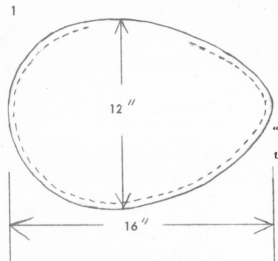

1

12 "

16 "

"Cut two oval pieces of canvas, or heavy muslin, . . ."

sand, or sawdust; wool scraps cut in ½″ x 1½″ pieces, firmly packed in the ham, are excellent for stuffing, but be sure they are colorfast. Slip-stitch opening by hand. If the ham becomes soft, just open the sides and add more filling. Sometimes a ham in smaller proportions is quite useful.

Sandbag Weights

Follow instructions for making the tailor's ham, but fill with clean white river sand, instead of wool. Make sizes ranging from 3″ squares to 10″ x 3″ rectangles.

Chemical Press Cloths

Specially treated cloths may be purchased in department stores or tailor supply stores. A soft, wool flannel cloth will raise the nap when used as press cloth for woolens. Be sure to use the right side of press cloth next to the wool. It is usually marked "This Side Up." Dampen with a sponge, then press with medium hot iron until thoroughly steamed. Do not press until completely dry or the material will become shiny.

When pressing worsted, gabardine, or other hard-surfaced material, use two press cloths. Place one on the material and sponge cloth thoroughly; then place the second one on top and press with medium iron, using a slow, rotating motion. Do not hold iron in same position on the wool for any length of time. Follow grain line of fabric whenever possible.

Use as much caution in pressing as you do in the actual construction of the garment. Any garment will lose its shape if pressed incorrectly. Wool is resilient and can be stretched and set with a very hot iron, or shrunk with too much water and heat.

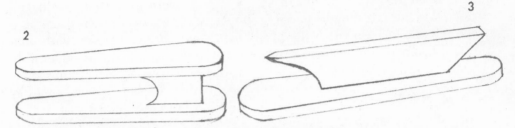

It is advisable to press after each sewing operation and, upon completion of garment, to send it to a cleaner, or tailor, for professional pressing and finishing. Professional pressing of your garment is a *must* if it is to fit properly.

Sleeve Board

A *sleeve board* is used for pressing sleeve seams open and shrinking fullness out of sleeve and garment seams around the armscye, but it may be used for more than pressing a sleeve. For custom tailoring, a sleeve board mounted on a sturdy hardwood base is preferable. If the base is covered, it may be used for pressing short seams as you put your garment together. *Note:* Do not overpad. Fig. 2.

Seam Board

Use the *seam board* to press seams of garment under construction. Fig. 3. Slightly dampen seams with the fingertips. Press firmly but do not hold the iron on the material more than a few seconds. If the seams are stubborn, press open, then apply dampness, and press again.

Novel Seam Board

This is especially useful for pressing silks or failles. Use a strip of unfinished, 1″ half-round, available from a lumber yard. Pad lightly with sheeting, or muslin, and tack each end to a flat board to keep the stick from rolling, Fig. 4. Use very fine finishing

nails to prevent splitting. This is excellent for pressing seams and particularly good for materials that spot —silk or faille—because the pressure of the iron is on the stitching and not on the raw edges of the seam.
Note: Be sure that all pressing seam boards are made of hardwood, especially parts that come in direct contact with the heat of the iron.

Velvet Board

Never attempt to press velvet unless you have a *velvet board*. This is a board with a series of fine steel wire bristles protruding from it. It may be used for pressing corduroys or soft woolens, as well as velvet. The nap fits between the wires and can be pressed without crushing or marking. Place the pile face down on the bristles and dampen lightly; press with a warm iron until dry. Fig. 5.

5

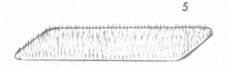

Hardwood Block

Any *hardwood block*, sanded smooth, with a handle inserted for convenient leverage, makes a nice pounding block. Fig. 6. A round-edged hardwood block is best for pressing curved seams, Fig. 7, or finished edges that should be straight. Butt against the hardwood block, dampen, and press. With patient persistence, this will straighten a curved seam. Repeat if necessary.

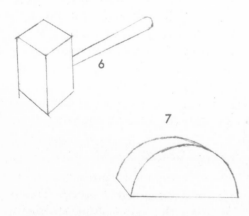

When pressing front edges and other finished seams, if razor-sharp finished seams are desired, press with a damp cloth until practically all moisture is removed; then place on a hardwood surface. Cover with thin cloth and pound seams vigorously with the hardwood block, until thoroughly dry. Repeat as many times as necessary to get thin, flat seams.

QUESTIONS

1. Name ten most necessary pieces of equipment.
2. Describe the tailor's ham and its function.
3. When do you use two press cloths? Why?
4. What is the function of a sleeve board?
5. Describe a seam, or edge board, and its use.
6. How do you press velvet?
7. How do you obtain sharp seam finishes?

Helpful Pressing Hints

Darts are used to mold, shape, or fit. It is important for a dart to retain the contour you have sewed into it. For best results, press on a tailor's ham.

Pressing Darts

When *pressing darts* in wool, slash and press open from center toward point. Do not slash to the point because this will weaken the dart. Large darts should not be slashed closer than within 1″ of the point. Press from center of the dart to each end before dampening, Fig. 8; then dampen and press thoroughly dry

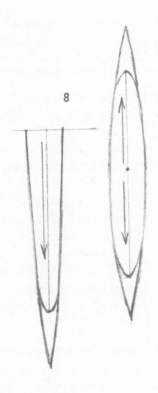

8

pressed as a box pleat, or to the center of the body. Cotton and rayon darts are treated like silk unless the material is heavy in weight; then treat like wool and overcast raw edges.

Let the size of the dart determine how far it should be slashed, or the amount to be trimmed away. When the material frays, overcast the raw edges where the darts are cut and pressed open.

A metal knitting needle inserted into the point of a dart helps in pressing.

How to Remove Shine Caused by Wear or Improper Pressing

Do not press worsted, gabardine, rayon failles, or bengalines with direct heat from a steam iron because these fabrics will take on a greater shine.

To reduce the shine on elbows, backs of skirts, and seats of trousers, wring out the press cloth in a solution of ¼ cup of white vinegar to 1 cup of water and steam press the affected spots. Repeat several times, but do not press thoroughly dry. After the garment has been pressed almost dry, take a stiff brush and raise the nap of the shiny area. In severe cases, gently rub the shiny surface with fine sandpaper.

To eliminate pleat and seam "indentations," slip tissue paper or heavy brown paper underneath the seam, or pleat, before pressing. Select the paper for pressing according to the weight and type of fabric.

from center to each end, on the seam board.

Small darts at the back, and skirt and sleeve darts, should also be slashed enough to stitch flat at seam junctions; then press like a box pleat, such as waist and skirt darts where they are joined together.

Darts that are closed from each end, such as the waist darts in jackets and coats, are treated in the same manner with the exception of slashing from the center to within 1″ of *each* end. Press from the center to each end on the edge board.

Silk darts should not be slashed open, except when in excess of ½″, but

How to Remove Scorch Stains

Make a solution of ½ cup of hydrogen peroxide, ½ cup water, and a few drops of household ammonia just before you are ready to use it. Sponge the scorch stains with the solution; then thoroughly rinse with clear water before pressing. If the first application doesn't remove stains, repeat and press with a cloth.

QUESTIONS

1. How are darts pressed in wool, in silk?
2. How do you press darts closed at both ends?
3. Explain the method of removing shine caused by wear and ironing.
4. How do you remove scorch stains?

Helpful Sewing Hints

Preparing Thread

Always cut thread from a spool on the bias. This makes threading easier.

To keep thread from tangling, place the end cut from the spool through the eye of the needle and knot the opposite end. Then pull across beeswax several times.

When knotting double thread, make two separate knots. This keeps the thread from twisting.

Correct Sewing Machine Posture

Sit with both feet flat on the floor, shoulders square and erect. Never sit on the edge of the chair when sewing but sit close enough to comfortably guide the fabric.

Pressure and Stitch Adjustment

The pressure on the presser foot is determined by the type and thickness of the fabric being sewn. Some machines have automatically adjusted pressure bars; others have to be adjusted manually. See your machine instruction book. Always test stitches on fabric scraps until the machine feeds smoothly and evenly.

Napped fabrics such as velvet, corduroy, and thick wools require light pressure. Thinner fabrics such as cottons, nylons, and silks, require heavier pressure.

When sewing very thick fabrics, a large stitch adjustment is necessary, with a medium to heavy size needle. Mercerized cotton thread requires a heavier needle than silk thread. When using finer synthetic fabrics, a smaller stitch and heavier pressure are required, with loose bobbin and top tension. Be sure to test all of these factors on the machine and fabric to be used, before sewing the garment.

Machine Sewing

Always pull both threads away from you, under the presser foot. Have the needle bar raised to its highest point before starting to sew, and the top and bottom thread long enough to hold with the thumb and forefinger of the left hand. This will prevent the thread from breaking, or knotting, on the wrong side.

Steady, fast sewing makes smoother, straighter seams than slower, choppy sewing.

Stitching Garment Seams

When sewing a garment together, baste all sections from top to bottom and machine stitch from bottom to top.

To tack threads at the beginning and end of a seam, release the pressure of the presser foot slightly with the forefinger of the left hand, holding the material with the thumb to keep it from moving along with the action of the feed dogs. By holding the material and allowing the needle to go slowly up and down in the same position, a knot is formed. This technique can be applied to any type of machine, whether it is foot or electric powered.

How to Square Corners

Do *not* sew to a corner and place the needle down to turn, as is often done. Stop about two stitches from the corner, stitch across it, then continue stitching down the seam. This method insures nicely squared corners. When pivoting on needle at the corners, a teepee shape is formed that cannot be finished professionally.

Removing Bastings

When pulling out basting threads, a crochet hook is a good tool to use.

Machine Care

After finishing sewing for the day, remove the bobbin from the carrier case and place a drop of oil in the case and in each opening that will take oil. Place a pad under the presser foot to absorb excess oil and lower the needle to hold the pad in place. This will help keep the machine in good operating condition.

QUESTIONS

1. Describe the correct method of threading a needle.
2. What is correct sewing posture?
3. What fabric adjustments are necessary on the sewing machine?
4. What is the best way to sew a straight seam?
5. How do you obtain square corners?
6. What care should your machine receive after sewing?

Hand-Tailoring Stitches

Tailor Tacking

Salvage yarn by unraveling an old sweater, and use this for *tailor tacking*. To remove kinks, wind the yarn on heavy cardboard and dip in cold water. Yarn entangles, causing the tacks to stay in place longer than thread. Mark dots on the fabric and remove pattern.

Thread the needle with a single strand of yarn (or a double strand of thread) and stitch through the garment pieces with a small stitch at the pattern marking; then back-stitch in the same marking, leaving about a 1″

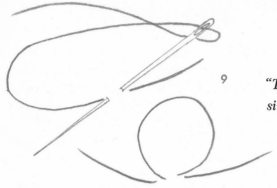

9

"Thread the needle with a single strand of yarn . . ."

thread loop. Fig. 9. Do not snip the thread loop. Move on to the next mark and repeat the back-stitch and loop. Thread the needle with a needle threader if you have trouble getting yarn in the eye of the needle. When making a series of tailor tacks, make running basting stitches with the thread eased between stitches. Stitch only at pattern dots. Fig. 10.

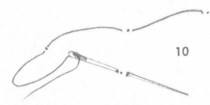

10

After the tailor tacks are in position, gently separate the two pieces of the garment and clip the threads between the pieces. By using this method, the tailor tacks are more likely to stay in place. When there is a series of guide marks close together, use different colored yarn to identify them—such as red for triangles, green for dots, and white for squares.

Tailor's Quilting or Padding Stitch

Tailor's quilting is done by working at the innermost point to the outside, or edge, of the garment. Take a small stitch, barely picking up the material underneath, pointing the needle toward the body. Drop down about ¼″ and repeat until the row is complete. Fig. 11. Do not change the position

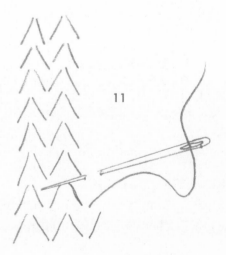

11

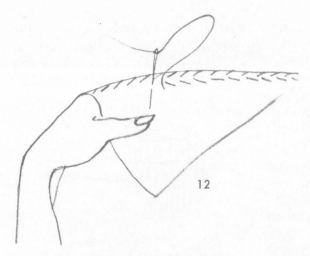

12

"Place padding area around the hand with four fingers together and the thumb on top, . . ."

of the material in the left hand. Work up and down until the padding is finished. When padding heavy coats, drop down about ½″ instead of ¼″.

Tailor's quilting must never be taut or the garment will have a puckered appearance. Place bulk of the garment on the knees. Place padding area around the hand with four fingers together and the thumb on top, with the raw edge facing the body. In padding toward a raw edge, the padding area will gradually unroll, Fig. 12. Keep a firm hold on the material all the time, but do not pull the thread tight. Do not hold padding area with the fingers on top of the fabric because this will cause it to curl in the opposite direction.

This is probably the least used yet the most necessary tailoring stitch for the custom tailored look.

Catch-stitch

Catch-stitching is fast and simple to do. Always stitch from *left* to *right*,

keeping the stitches even and loose. Take a running basting stitch, drop down, and repeat. Fig. 13. When using as permanent stitching, barely

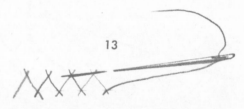

13

pick up the fabric so stitches will be invisible. *Remember:* Work from left to right. Keep your stitches staggered evenly for neatness and strength, and firm but not taut.

This stitch is used extensively in tailoring because of the freedom it assures, while at the same time it firmly anchors sections together.

Feather Stitch

The *feather stitch*, a lock stitch, is used for trim and durability. It is used in finishing pleats in garment linings, hems of skirts, etc. Many years ago it was called "briar stitch" and used extensively in embroidery work.

One might call this stitch a fancy catch-stitch because it is executed the same way, except that the feather stitch is worked from *right* to *left*, always throwing the thread in *front* of the needle. The size of the pick-up stitch determines the appearance of the feather stitch. Feather stitching is stronger than catch-stitching because each stitch locks itself. Fig. 14.

over and under each thread on the cross grain until the hole is completely darned, Fig. 15. Work the end of the thread into the fabric about ½″

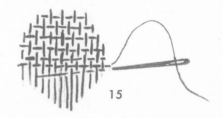

15

inside the damaged section. Place the darned section on a padded board and hammer (Fig. 6) to blend the thread

14

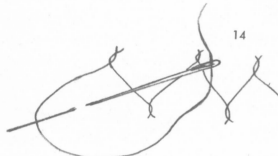

". . . the feather stitch is worked from right to left, . . ."

Darning Holes or Cuts

Sometimes accidents occur when cutting or wearing clothes and there is no commercial weaver available. To *darn*, pull a thread from a seam of the garment, or from a scrap of the material, and thread a small needle. Start to weave the thread about ½″ away from the cut or tear; do not tack, or knot, as the woolen fibers will blend together. Weave back and forth *with* the grain of the material until the hole is closed; then weave

fibers. Place the material in a small embroidery hoop for easier darning.

When darning novelty weaves, try to follow the weave of the fabric.

Basting Stitches

The *basting stitch* is a small, even stitch, approximately ⅛″ long. This stitch is used as a temporary means of keeping sections together for fitting and machine stitching. A No. 5 in-between needle makes basting easier and keeps stitches uniform, Fig. 16.

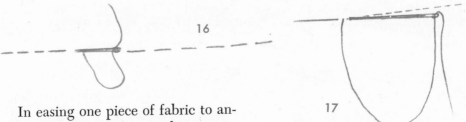

16

17

In easing one piece of fabric to another, sleeve to armscye, be sure to keep basting stitches very small so the ease will stay in place.

Backstitch

The *backstitch* is used where strong basting is required, or when matching checks and stripes. It is more work than the basting stitch but pays dividends in the finished garment. Place a running basting stitch inside the stitching line to hold the fabric in place. Backstitch parallel to the first basting, checking to be sure stripes or checks are matched. The length of this stitch is determined by the weight of the material. First, take a running stitch and pull the thread through; then go back, putting the needle in at the end of the preceding stitch. Bring the needle out so this stitch is twice as long as the first stitch. Repeat the process with long stitches underneath and short ones on top. Do not overlap top stitches.

This stitch is done with buttonhole twist, instead of using stay tape, to reinforce neck and armscye seams, and to eliminate bulk. Fig. 17.

Uneven Basting

Uneven basting is used when shirr-

ing, or small pleating, is done by hand; also, when basting or anchoring seams together temporarily.

Take ½" stitches on top and small stitches on bottom. Use heavy thread and keep the stitches uniform when shirring or pleating. The result is a professional looking finish when the material is padded, not shirred, before stitching by machine, Fig. 18.

18

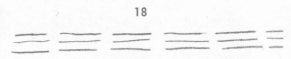

Make two or three rows of basting; then shirr or draw together. Machine stitch on inside of basting. Tighten the basting thread and leave in permanently. When table basting this is a fast, easy method of joining two pieces together.

Overhanding or Nappery Stitch

Overhanding or *nappery stitching* is seldom used in tailoring unless you are hemming a linen scarf or tie, or table linens. Overhanding makes a strong stitch.

"Press the fold of the hem, then crease between the thumb and . . ."

19

Press the fold of the hem, then crease between the thumb and forefinger. Pull the needle straight through the hem and material, but do not make it too tight or the hem will not smooth out, Fig. 19. This hem must be done with small stitches about ⅛″ apart, barely picking up the material and hem. Slip the needle in the crease of hem to keep the thread invisible between stitches.

Right Side Basting or Slip-basting

To *right side baste* or *slip-baste*, press seam to form a crease. Overlap pressed seam on unpressed section and pin close together, matching stripes or checks. Make sure the pin enters at the crease and picks up the seam margin, so that pieces can be opened up for basting. Fig. 20.

When matching patterned fabric, top baste as shown on diagram, Fig.

21, catching crease of the seam margin on the sewing line.

If you are not using top basting, open up and baste in the crease of the pressed seam on the wrong side. If the material is heavy, back stitch at each stripe, or check, to keep material from slipping when machine stitching.

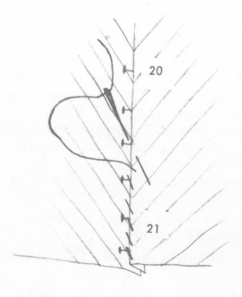

20

21

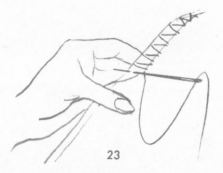

23

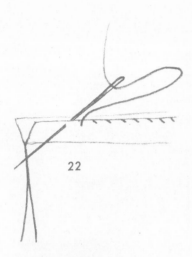

22

Overcasting

Overcasting is compulsory in fabrics that ravel or fray easily. Trim seam margins evenly, enter the needle underneath about ⅛" from the raw edge, then bring it through and over the fabric again in the same direction. Hence, the name overcast, Fig. 22. The old-fashioned method was to double seam, or French seam, which does not give as smooth an appearance as overcasting.

Rolled Edge Finish

A *rolled edge finish* is used for hand-finished hems on dress ties, scarfs, tie sashes, and baby clothes made of sheer fabrics—crepe, chiffon, batiste, and voile.

Machine stitch as close as possible to the raw edge of the hem. Crease the hem edge on the machine stitching line, between thumb and forefinger.

Using a small needle, with fine silk

thread begin alternating stitches; i.e., place needle into machine stitching, take a very small stitch, and then barely pick up fabric thread in the article being hemmed. Fig. 23. Continue these alternating stitches, one into machine stitching and one into fabric, in 1 or 2 inch sections; then draw thread taut to form a rolled hem. Fig. 24.

Buttonhole Stitch

The *buttonhole stitch* is rarely used because the modern sewing machine

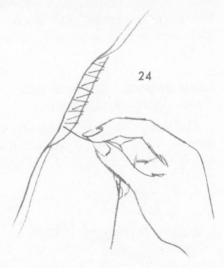

24

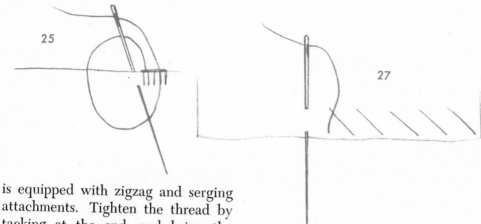

25

27

is equipped with zigzag and serging attachments. Tighten the thread by tacking at the end, and bring the needle through the wrong side at the desired depth. Throw the thread over the point of the needle; then bring the needle straight through the material, keeping the purl knot on top, Fig. 25. Do not pull the thread too tight and remember to keep all the stitches even.

Serging is a close overcasting done by a special machine, and used on the edges of rugs, carpets, and some factory-made garments. The zigzag attachment does an adequate imitation of serging.

Lazy Daisy or Chain Stitch (False Buttonhole Stitch)

The *lazy daisy* or *chain stitch* is used to finish lapel or sleeve buttonholes. Enter fabric as if to take a

26

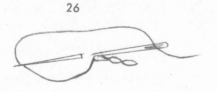

small basting stitch. Loop thread around the needle, pulling needle through the loop. This forms a petal-like stitch. Bring the needle through the fabric at the wide end of the petal and repeat the previous stitch to form a chain-like finish, Fig. 26.

Diagonal Stitch

The *diagonal stitch* is frequently used in the second row of edge basting, because it is fast and firm. This stitch is useful in keeping the edges of the garment from rolling to the right side while it is in the construction stage, and for holding several layers of fabric together.

Enter the needle in horizontal position and drop down about ½″ or more, depending on the weight of the material. Tack stitch at the beginning and end in place of a knot because this stitch does not pull out very easily, Fig. 27. The fastest, easiest method to do this stitch is to table baste. Keep the edge of the garment

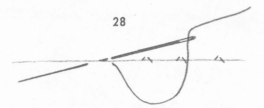

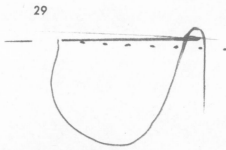

cupped over your hand, or the edge of the table, in order to curl the seams in the right direction.

Slip Stitch

The *slip stitch* is perferred if it is necessary to fell linings with invisible hand sewing.

Place the needle under the fold of the material and gently pick up one or two threads; then move the needle down the crease of material and pick up a few more threads. Fig. 28. When using in hems, keep stitches loose so they are invisible on the right side of garment. They should be used where there is no strain on them.

Saddle-stitching or Pick-stitching

Use buttonhole twist thread a shade darker than the garment.

Make a loose backstitch, keeping the small stitch on the right side. Place stitches the desired width from finished edge.

Catch into all the seam thickness but keep stitches visible on right side of garment only, Fig. 29. If stitch trim is desired on the underside of coat front, repeat process on the underside.

Drapery Basting

Drapery basting is used to attach linings to draperies. It is especially useful in attaching interfacings of collars, cuffs, and fronts on fine sheer fabrics, because it is completely invisible.

Apply this stitch to a garment, baste lining or interfacing to top fabric at innermost point. Catch-stitch interfacing to top fabric, minus seam allowance. Separate the two pieces and work within ¼″ or ½″ of the catch-stitched portion from the left end of the article to the right end. When the row is completed, begin another row, working in the same manner. Rows should be ¼″ to ½″ apart, and individual stitches should be the same distance apart. Fig. 30, page 30.

In draperies, the rows of stitches are vertical from the top to about 6″ from the hem line. Rows should be 6″ apart, and worked from the outside to the center of the window. Individual stitches should also be 6″ apart.

Stab Stitching

Stab stitching is stabbing the

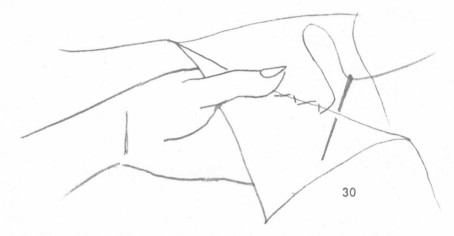

needle downward and then upward through a heavy thickness of fabric, and is used most often in attaching shoulder pads and sewing on buttons.

QUESTIONS

1. What is tailor tacking and how is it used?
2. Explain tailor padding.
3. Describe the difference between catch-stitch and feather stitch.
4. Where are small basting stitches necessary?
5. Where is the back stitch used in preference to the basting stitch?
6. What are uses for the uneven basting stitch?
7. Where is the nappery stitch used in tailoring?
8. When is it necessary to right side baste?
9. What is the function of overcasting? Why is it preferable to French seams?
10. Where is the rolled edge finish used?
11. Explain the buttonhole, serging, and zigzag stitches.
12. Where is the lazy daisy or chain stitch used?
13. Where is the diagonal stitch necessary? Why?
14. Where is the slip stitch frequently applied?
15. What kind of thread is used for saddle stitching?
16. Explain two uses for drapery basting.
17. When is stab stitching used most often?

Types of Seams

Double Mitered Seams

Double mitered seams are used when binding is desired on topside and underside of garment. Fold together and cut away corner, or stitch and then cut away. This is used in bias binding or any kind of edge-trimming in suits and dresses. To simplify attaching of binding, press seam allowance before sewing by hand or machine.

When the binding is in one piece,

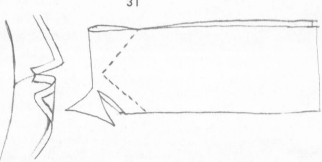

31

"Fold together and cut away corner, or stitch ..."

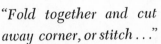

stitch and cut away on the inside and outside seam at mitered corners. Crease the binding in the center and then press seam open before joining to garment. Fig. 31. Trim corners and baste. When an invisible finish is desired, stitch in crease of pressed seam. When top stitching is desired, stitch on crease at right side of garment. Either slip-stitch or machine stitch other edge of binding.

Single Mitered Seams

Single mitered seams are treated much the same as double mitered seams. Bring facings over to stitching line of center front. A binding one-half the width of the double mitered binding is used and applied as top trim instead of being used to bind the edge. The facing is brought right to the stitching line of the underside. Fig. 32.

Plain Basting Seam

To *baste* a seam, place the two sections on the table. Be sure they are perfectly smooth, because wool fibers have a tendency to cling together. Smoothing wool on a flat surface would cause fibers to intertwine. In working with wool, hold the two sections up at the stitching line and separate with a yardstick so that fabric will hang evenly.

When pinning fabric together before basting, place the pins at right angles instead of parallel with the seams so they can be left while working. Fig. 33.

32

33

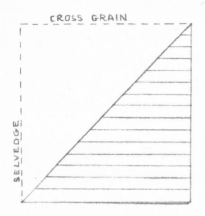

34

CROSS GRAIN

SELVEDGE

How to Make Bias Binding

True bias, the diagonal grain of the material, is found by bringing the cross grain to meet the selvedge, or straight grain. Cutting on the fold thus created provides true bias. Fig. 34. It will have the greatest "give" or stretch, and the most graceful drape. One yard of material will make approximately 36 yards of 1 inch bias binding.

Begin by cutting a true square. Cut on the cross grain, parallel to the straight grain. Cut the square diagonally on the true bias line.

In order to form a tube from which the bias binding may be cut in one piece, join lengthwise grain edges. Fig. 35. Then join the cross grain edges together, letting the width of the bias desired extend where sewn together. Fig. 36. Press seams open.

Start cutting bias strip with the extended portion; cut around and around until the end of the tube is

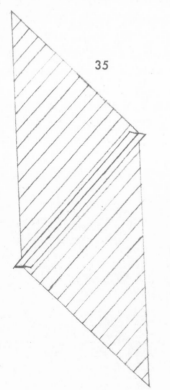

35

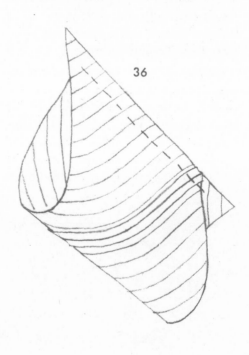

36

37

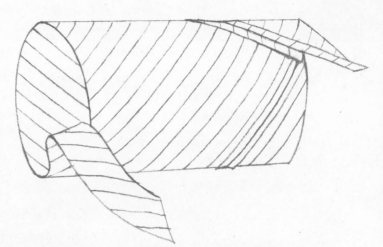

". . . cut around and around until the end of the tube is reached."

reached. Fig. 37. This is a quick way to make a lot of bias binding out of small pieces of material. You can apply this method to any size square of material.

Bound Seam with Finished Top and Bottom Edges

This seam is used extensively in unlined jackets, men's summer suits, and ladies' raincoats with half linings. A seam can be bound with a machine binder attachment, using commercial seam binding or binding prepared as in previous instructions, so that lining and bindings match.

When binding with seam tape without the machine binding attachment, baste binding around raw edge of seam with the underneath part slightly wider than the right side. Machine stitch as close to the edge as possible, on the right side. The underside of the tape will be caught by the stitches because it is wider.

Binding Seams with Raw Edge Bias

This seam is more work but neater and stronger than a seam bound with commercial binding. Unfinished bias binding may be purchased in rolls from tailor supply establishments. However, these rolls may not match the lining perfectly. When a perfect color match is desired, make bias from lining fabric, using previous instructions.

Place the right side of the binding to the right side of the garment seam. It isn't necessary to baste or pin unless desired, but care must be taken not to stretch the seams.

Stitch about ⅛″ from edge, keeping the seam straight; then press on the right side of binding. Fold under the extended bias binding, or wrap around the raw edge of seams, and baste. Edge-stitch the binding to the seam allowance from the right side.

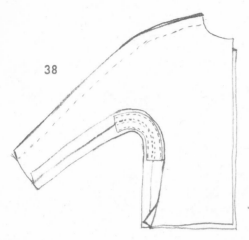

38

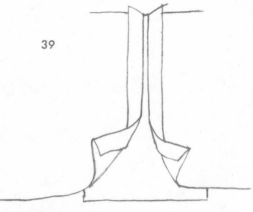

39

Corded Seams

Corded seams make a beautiful, chic trim for classic suits and tailored dresses. Make bias tape according to previous instructions. Heavy twine makes a nice size cording for dresses and lightweight suits. Yarn may also be used effectively.

Place cord in the center fold of bias and stitch with a cording foot, close to cord. Baste the covered cord to the seams, with raw edges flush with one section, and stitch inside the previous stitching. Ease the cording around corners and curves slightly. Then baste the other section on top with right sides facing and machine stitch slightly closer to cording, using the previous stitching as a guide. Fig. 40. Blend seams after sections are joined together. Clip to stitching line in three or four places around curves. This same method is used in making slipcovers for furniture.

Top-stitched or Welt Seam

A *top-stitched* or *welt seam* is used

Reinforcing Seams with Tape

Dolman, raglan, or kimono sleeves, cut in one piece, should be reinforced, by hand or by machine, with silk from lining or hem tape, *not* bias. This type of sleeve should be reinforced at the underarm seam. Fig. 38. Long sleeves should also be reinforced at the shoulder seam.

Slot Seams

A *slot seam* is quite often used in tailoring for trim of contrasting color. Baste and press the regular seam allowances and join or baste to the underlay, butted together or revealing as much contrasting fabrics as desired.

Machine stitch about ¼″ from the pressed seam, keeping seams as straight as possible. If garment lining covers the slot seam, leave as is; if not, bind the edges or overcast by hand. This seam may be stitched any width desired. Fig. 39.

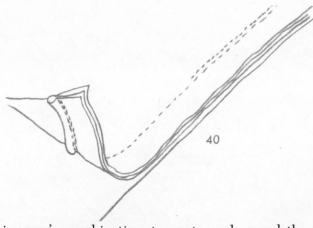

40

*"Place cord in the center
fold of bias and stitch ..."*

in men's combination topcoats and raincoats, or ladies' sport and casual clothing. It is made on the *inside* of the garment.

Join together as for any plain seam, and machine stitch. Press seams to-

41

42

ward the *front* of the garment. This makes them more weatherproof. Trim the underneath seam as wide as desired for the finished seam, Fig. 41, and top stitch accordingly. Fig. 42. This narrow underseam acts as a filler for the welt seam.

When stitching around curves, clip the underseam and top seam margin; then top stitch.

To be accurate in gauging a seam width, place a guide basting along stitching line or the garment will have a crude appearance. When this seam is used in unlined garments, bind the extended raw edge with bias seam binding.

Flat Felled Seam

The *flat felled seam* is similar to the welt seam, except that it is finished on the *right side* of the garment. This seam is popular for making sport shirts, pajamas, and ladies' lingerie.

Join the seams together with wrong sides of material facing. Trim the underneath seam as wide as the finished seam should be. When finishing seams

35

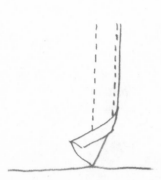

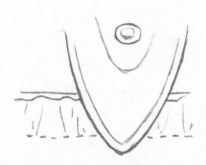

on the right side, press toward the *back* of the garment.

Fold the top seam over the underseam and baste, pin, or machine stitch on the edge of the fold. Fig. 43. When stitching on a curve, clip underseam and folded portion of top seam slightly, to relieve strain.

Edge Stitched Seam

An *edge stitched seam* is used in

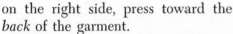

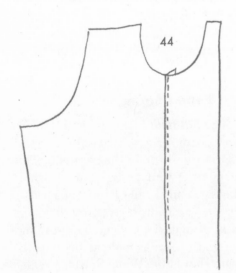

place of binding when the material is sheer or loosely woven.

Close the seams in the regular manner, and press open or flat. Turn under the raw edge ⅛″ or ¼″, depending on the weight of the material. Stitch close to the crease edge of the seam margin, not into the garment, using loose machine stitches.

Flat-stitching for Seams or Facings

Flat-stitching is necessary on facings, cuffs, or undercollars, to conceal finished seams. To do this, lay seams toward facing and top stitch on the facing, close to stitching line. Fig. 44. This eliminates pressing and insures the seam's rolling to the underside of the garment.

Easing Fullness Into Seam

To *ease fullness into a seam,* baste with the eased part of the seam on top, curved over the left hand, and the smooth side on the bottom. The material will automatically ease in when curved over the fingers, because the thumb holds it in that position. For this reason, the thumb is commonly called "the material thief" by tailors. Use small, uniform stitches when easing fullness. Dampen seam margins, keeping them together, and shrink out *before* machine stitching. Fig. 45. Press at right angles to seam, *not with seam*, on board, or over ham. When easing fullness into jersey or other stretchy material, machine stitch the seam binding in seam, or catch-stitch to seams, by hand after they have been pressed open.

Straight and Bias Material Joined Together

Baste the bias material on top of the straight, with small even stitches, placing it on a flat surface in order to distribute the bias fabric evenly. Baste from shoulder to hemline and machine stitch from hemline to shoulder line. The following is a good rule to follow if easing is required: Place the fuller portion of fabric next to the machine feeder. The feeder normally eases lower material to the top layer of material.

Gussets Inserted in Seams

A *gusset* is a triangular piece of material, inserted in a garment to give added width or strength. You can do it! The secret of smooth fitting gussets is to avoid stitching beyond seam junctions of a garment.

Machine stitch with small stitches

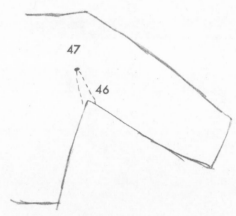

around the slash outline to strengthen, before inserting gussets. Fig. 46. Stitch inside the seam allowance to keep this stitching invisible. Bar tack at the tip of the slash, on wrong side, to reinforce the garment. Fig. 47.

Join the gusset to the front of the garment, Fig. 48. Join backs and fronts together, from hemline to gusset junction, and from sleeve edge to gusset junction. Stitch only to the gusset seam junctions, *not* across them. See page 38.

After sleeve and body sections are joined together, join the gusset to the back of garment by stitching up to the seam junction. Keep your seam allowances the same at garment and gusset junction. Tack the stitches, or pull threads to the wrong side and tie.

Barely catch the material of the garment in slashed corners to prevent puckering. Machine stitch with the gusset section facing the feeder of the machine. When you turn corners in gussets, pivot on the machine needle instead of stitching two or three

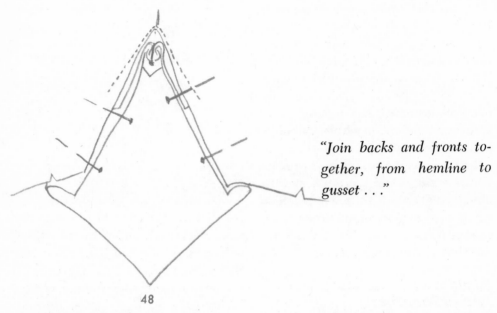

*"Join backs and fronts to-
gether, from hemline to
gusset . . ."*

48

stitches across the corner. Be sure reinforcement stitches do not show on
the right side when completed.

Press the gusset seams open, then
back together and away from the gusset. After gussets have been pressed,
the edge of the garment along the
gusset may be top stitched. Fig. 49.

*"Press the gusset seams open,
then back together . . ."*

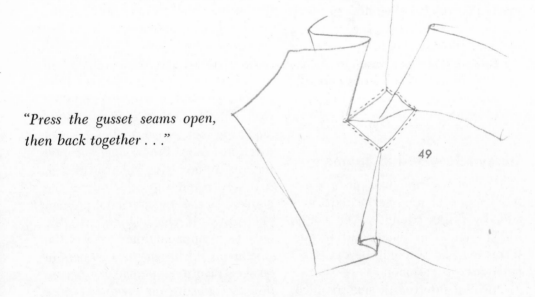

49

When the gusset is in two pieces (front and back), join each to its respective section and finish as in the instructions on page 37. Sew the underarm seam from hem to sleeve edge.

Some gussets extend under the arm and form part of the sleeve. Treat as in previous instructions.

Gussets should always be reinforced. Place the bar tack on the wrong side at the point of the gusset, by barely picking into the garment, to keep stitches invisible on the right side. This type of reinforcement eliminates bulk.

QUESTIONS

1. What are double mitered seams? Where are they used?
2. How does the single mitered seam differ from the double?
3. Where is plain basting normally used?
4. Explain bias binding and how it is made.
5. Where are bound seams with finished top and bottom edges used?
6. Why is bias binding with raw edge desirable?
7. What types of seams should be reinforced with tape?
8. Explain slot seams.
9. How is cording made? Where is it used?
10. Where is the top-stitched seam most commonly used?
11. Where is the flat felled seam used? How does it differ from the top-stitched or welt seam?
12. Where is edge stitching used?
13. Explain flat-stitching and its use.
14. How do you ease fullness into a seam?
15. Explain how a bias section and a straight section should be joined.
16. What is the function of a gusset?
17. Describe the steps used in inserting and pressing gussets.
18. Are gussets reinforced?

Inserting Slide Fasteners

Placket Slide Fasteners

The following method may be applied to skirts and dresses: Close the side seam to where the slide fastener tape will start, using regular seam allowance.

Dip the slide fastener in water and let it dry for shrinkage.

On the back of the skirt or dress, baste or press a fold in the seam allowance ⅛" inside stitching line where front and back of the skirt have been joined together, in the seam margin.

Open the pull tab on the slide fastener and allow seam allowance plus length of pull tab before basting in place. Fig. 50. Baste ⅛" fold of skirt back seam close to the slide fastener, and machine stitch. See page 40.

Do not ease or stretch the wool when basting to the slide fastener tape. Continue stitching a ⅛" tuck in the seam margin about 1" below the end of the slide fastener tape when joining it to the back of the garment, Fig. 51. See page 40.

When using heavier weight fabrics, sew a piece of bias silk 1½" wide to the front seam of the skirt, as long as

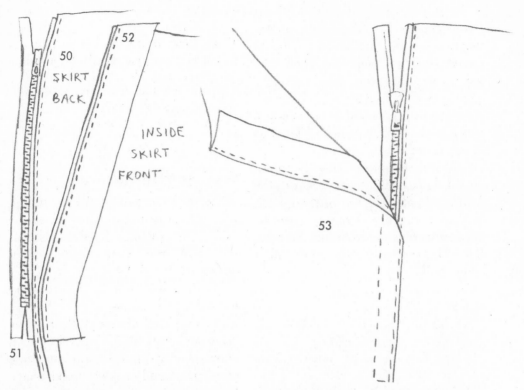

the slide fastener. For lighter fabrics, use the garment material for bias facing.

Remove bastings of skirt seams and join bias to skirt by continuous seam stitching.

Turn skirt and facing seam margin toward facing, and flat stitch close to edge of the facing on the right side, Fig. 52. (Refer to Flat-stitching, page 36.) Blend seams slightly. Turn bias to inside, and baste right skirt seam allowance over back skirt section, keeping the ⅛″ overlap where the slide fastener was attached. Be sure the bias strip facing rolls slightly underneath to remain invisible from the right side.

Carefully baste the front of the garment so the slide fastener is concealed when closed. The fastener tape should be ⅛″ inside the placket except at the top. Fig. 53. Fan out slightly at top on the skirt front to allow for the pull tab. Place a second row of basting near the slide fastener on the skirt front. Keep basting straight so it can be used as a guide for either machine stitching or hand-finishing. Press over tailor's ham and machine stitch from either the right or wrong side, preferably the right side, from the bottom of the slide fastener towards the waist. Remove bastings which close skirt sections and stitch close to the lock; then lift presser foot, slide lock down, and finish the seam. Slide fasteners can be inserted in this manner without attaching the slide fastener foot if caution is exercised when sewing.

Finish the bottom of placket straight, or angular, and press.

Sometimes hand-stitching rather than machine stitching is desired for closing the placket. When this is done, use hand picking. (See Stitch Section, page 29.)

Slide Fasteners in Neck Seams

Close the seam to the end of the slide fastener. From there on, close the neck opening with the largest stitch on the machine, and press the seam open.

Baste slide fastener to the seam with the slide exactly in center of seam opening. Allow enough ease in seams so fabric will meet and completely cover slide fastener when completed. Machine stitch across bottom of the tape and then up to the neckline on each side, staying as close to the fastener as possible. After the fastener is in, finish neck with facing, or binding. Finish the fastener at least 1″ below neck opening and fasten with hook and loop. (Refer to Corded Button

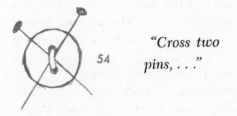

54   *"Cross two
pins, . . ."*

Loops or Thread Loops, pages 42 and 43.)

Placket slide fasteners also give the garment a finely tailored finish when used for neck openings.

QUESTIONS

1. Describe steps in inserting a slide fastener.
2. What stitch is used in hand-finishing a slide fastener?
3. How do you press slide fasteners?

Buttons, Fastenings, and Decorative Trim

Sewing on Buttons Correctly

Thread the needle with buttonhole twist, then pull thread over a piece of beeswax. Pull thread across a warm iron to melt wax; this will prevent a fabric stain. The beeswax strengthens the thread and keeps it from tangling. Use approximately the length of thread needed for sewing on one button. It is better to discard a small piece of thread than to have to re-thread the needle while sewing on a button.

Take one stitch through right side of material and tack or pull knot between layers of fabric where button will be attached. Bring needle through the eye of button. Cross two pins, barely catching material at button markings. Fig. 54. A kitchen match or six-penny nail may be used. Fig. 55. Pull the needle through the eye of the button down into the garment, all the way through, barely

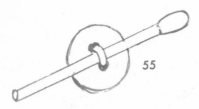

55

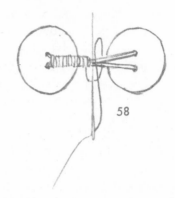

58

catching the lower layer of fabric; then, back up into the other eye of the button, over, and down into the top material.

Make about four stitches through the button, the top layer, and the interfacing of the garment. Starting at the base of the button, and finishing at the fabric, wrap thread around button tightly, forming a shank, which will hold the button upright. The shank should be a little longer than the thickness of the buttonhole opening, or approximately ⅛″ to ¼″, depending on thickness of area around buttonhole. Fig. 56. Pull the thread through the button shank twice, forming a cross, and knot. Fig. 57. Slip needle between top layer and facing, working over to finished seam, and tack firmly before clipping thread. The button shank should

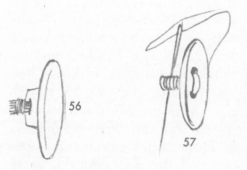

56

57

form an even, firm post. It should be uniform in thickness from base to the button eye. Buttons sewn on in this manner are always much stronger, regardless of the fabric used.

Link Buttons

To make link buttons, for French cuffs, collars, etc., join buttons together with at least six strands of thread. Work over these strands with a buttonhole or blanket stitch. See page 27. Use thread matching the garment with which link buttons will be worn. Fig. 58.

How to Make Thread Loops

To make button and hook loops, thread needle with double, or quadruple, strands of thread, and slip needle through the material, forming a loop on the underside as well as the top of the fabric. The top loop should have ease in it and the underneath loop should lie flat. Do this several times through the material.

Buttonhole stitch on the top loop, forming carrier. Fig. 59. Tack thread

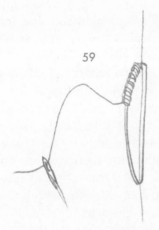

59

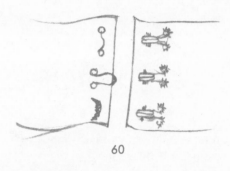

60

at the opposite end, slip thread between layers of material, and clip on underside.

To make a belt loop, chain crochet with several strands of the thread with which the garment was machine stitched. Pull through the side seams with the crochet hook and knot firmly on the wrong side. Make the knot large enough to prevent its working through the material to the outside of the garment.

This type loop is necessary for professional looking belts, buttons, or hook loops.

French Tacks

French tacks are used to anchor together two sections of a garment, leaving some ease—for example, coat linings at sides to keep fullness where it belongs, to keep large collars and cuffs in place, and to attach linings to draperies. To work French tacks, see instructions for Link Buttons, page 42.

Hooks and Eyes

There are two types of eyes to be used with hooks. The straight or bar type is used when edges overlap; the round or loop eye when edges come together. Place hook on the right side of the opening approximately ¹⁄₁₆″ off the edge. Using waxed or linen thread, stitch at eyes and tongue of hook with an overcasting stitch. Do not pull threads too taut. Rub clay chalk on the tongue of the hook so that when edges of the closing meet, a mark will be left where the eye, or hand-worked loop, should be placed. Sew eye in place, using overcasting stitch, or make a hand-worked loop the same as for a belt carrier. Fig. 60.

Corded Button Loops

To prepare *corded button loops,* refer to cording instructions, page 32. To determine the size of loop needed, draw a line on paper and place a button on the line. Loop cording around the button, and draw a perpendicular mark on the line, each side of the loop. Clip into inner bend of loop and

repeat, making as many loops as necessary. Hold loops in place with a darning needle, or a heavy basting needle, while machine stitching to opening. Fig. 61.

Snaps

The socket side of the snap goes on the overlap of garment; the ball part on the underlap. Sew the ball end of the snap in place, using overcasting stitch. Rub ball with clay chalk to mark spot where socket end of snap should be placed. Be sure stitches are invisible from outside of garment. Use snaps when there is no tension.

Finishing Scallops in Wool

If material is very heavy, face the wrong side with taffeta to eliminate as much of the bulk as possible. When basting, have the wool on top and curved over the hand. This automatically eases the wool onto the facing so it is invisible when finished.

Baste the seam margin of scallops evenly, with small stitches. Machine stitch with small stitches, using the basting for a guide. Clip all the way to the stitching in between scallops; trim the material a scant ¼″, and the facing a little narrower. Machine

stitch scallops with a medium small stitch. Turn to right side and roll out scallop seam, evenly and smoothly. Edge-baste before pressing. Press lightly, remove bastings, then press firmly for a finishing touch.

All scallops finish more smoothly and neatly if interfaced. Cut seam margin away and baste to wrong side of garment; then catch-stitch around scallops. Let lower edge of interfacing hang free. Machine stitch the facing to the garment, but don't stitch into interfacing.

Tubing

Fold bias material in half and stitch ¼″ or ½″ from fold, depending on the size of the finished tube.

Stretch the raw edge of tubing as you machine stitch to keep stitches from breaking when you turn the tubing right side out.

Thread needle with heavy thread and tighten at one end of tube; then slip needle through the tube, eye first, gently pulling on the thread until the tube is turned right side out. Do not trim seams too narrow or tubing will be limp. Allow seams to be same width as finished tubing. The seam margin acts as a filler for the tubing. If firmer tubing is desired, fill with yarn.

Another method is to tack a heavy thread at the end of the tubing and stitch this thread inside tubing, then pull thread to turn right side out. The tubing can be used for trim and frog fasteners.

Corded Bias Tubing for Belts or Button Loops

Make your bias strips wide enough to cover cording, plus seam allowance. It is better to trim the seams after sewing than to have them too narrow. Use cording, or half machine foot. Fold bias over cord and stitch close to the cord. Always have the cord longer than bias because bias stretches. In making corded belts, have cord one-third longer than finished belt will be. Stitch cord and bias together at one end, with cord extending the length of the finished belt, and tack two or three times.

Do not make stitches too small or they will stretch the material as you sew. Trim excess seams away, then work the tubing over the cord. When using for belts, tie a knot in each end and tuck raw edges inside. Then blind stitch by hand.

Corded tubing may be used for frog fasteners for suits and dresses, for button loops, or for trimming.

For professional looking frogs, or button loops, keep the seam edge of the cord to the inside because the outside stretches and curves more easily.

Trapunto or Quilted Design Trimming

This type of trimming is popular on classic dressmaker suits. Draw the outlines of the design where desired. Trapunto quilting is faced with net or other lightweight material on the wrong side. Outline the design by hand or machine, with a double row of stitching, approximately $\frac{1}{8}''$ or $\frac{1}{4}''$ apart, catching onto the underfacing. Thread needle with wool yarn or heavy cotton thread. Use filler of same fiber as the garment. Pull through outline to give a raised effect to the design. Cross the padding thread at the places where it forms the most pleasing design. Fig. 62. Tack ends of filler thread to the underfacing to hold in place. More than one strand of filler yarn may be necessary in order to give the design a raised effect.

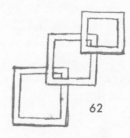

62

Plain Quilted Design

Baste thin cotton sheet wadding between a facing and the wrong side of the garment. Put design inside embroidery hoops and quilt by hand with small even stitches, catching through cotton sheet wadding, lining, and top fabric. Pull all ends of thread through to the wrong side and tighten. Catch-stitch facing of design to seam to keep it invisible. *Always use thread which matches the garment* for this trimming.

45

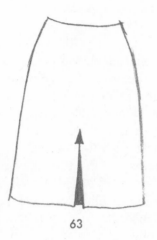

63

Contrast Trim at Shoulders and Hips

An original design may be created by unusual trim of bound slashes, inserted contrasting material, or underlay. Velveteen, velvet, and satin are good trims for this purpose. Here are a few illustrations:

Fig. 63. Skirt with contrasting underlay, and hand-worked arrow.

Fig. 64. Box pleat with contrasting underlay, and hand-worked arrow.

Fig. 65. Faced dart with contrasting underlay.

Fig. 66. Faced dart with contrasting underlay; closed in dart faced with contrasting underlay; and two types of collar trim.

Fig. 67. Notched cuff with underlay and hand-worked arrow, and sleeve with contrast extension below elbow.

Fig. 68. Slot seams with underlay trim at yoke and bodice.

Fig.' 69. Contrasting underlay of faced skirt darts, and welt extensions.

Make slot seams, or false pockets, with matching or contrasting material.

Cut darts away and face; then

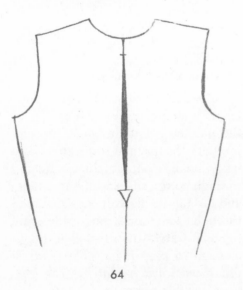

64

65

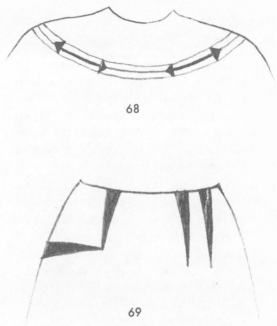

68

69

66

catch-stitch together and place under-lay on facing. If *contrasting fabric* is to be an underlay, use garment fabric for facing. If *facing* is to be of con-trasting fabric, underlay should be of the garment fabric. Top stitch any width seam you desire. Hand-worked arrows are very attractive on this type of seam.

QUESTIONS

1. Describe how buttons are sewn on. What kind of thread is used?

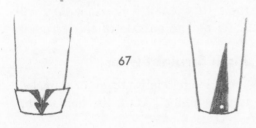

67

2. What is the function of link buttons?
3. How are thread loops made? Why are they desirable?
4. Where do you use French tacks?
5. On what sections of a garment are the hooks placed?
6. How are hooks and eyes matched?
7. How are corded button loops made and spaced?
8. Describe the placement of snaps.
9. Explain the construction of scallops.
10. How should bias tubing seams be trimmed?
11. What piece of equipment is neces-sary to make corded belts?
12. How long must a belt cord be?
13. Explain the construction of trapunto quilting. Where is it used?
14. What is the difference between plain quilted design and trapunto quilting?
15. What kind of material is used in contrast trim? Where is it most often applied?

47

Silk or linen thread is recommended for hems because of its strength. Cotton or mercerized cotton is not quite as strong but is very effective for washable garments. When using cotton thread, rub over beeswax, which will strengthen it as well as keep it from tangling.

Seam tape is rarely used in custom tailoring, unless especially preferred by the individual. Sometimes raw edges will fray, but properly finished seam edges are very durable.

For garments and skirts of bulky fabrics, underhemming is recommended. See instructions in this section, pages 51 and 52.

The first step in hemming a skirt is to mark the length. This may be determined in different ways, but two of the most popular methods are:

1. Measure from waist to crease of hem with skirt over the ironing board. Increase length slightly in the back, or front, if necessary. This requires some experimenting to determine where the additions are necessary.

2. Have someone mark the length with a marker. There are several markers available, but the old standby is the yardstick.

Note: Always wear a foundation garment and the type of shoes to be worn with the skirt when the hem is being marked.

Hems in Fully Lined Garments

After the length of the skirt has been marked with pins or chalk, crease-baste on marked line, including skirt and lining. Crease-baste hem, using contrasting thread on the marked line. Fig. 70. Pin or baste raw edge of hem to skirt and try on

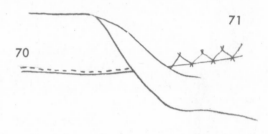

to check length. Press crease of hem with up and down motion of iron to avoid stretching fabric. Remove bastings, open hem, and trim lining away at crease of hem. Catch-stitch lining to hem crease of skirt with large stitches. Fig. 71. Trim hem; turn evenly. In straight skirts, 2½″ is a good width; 1″ to 1½″ for circular or bias cut skirts. Fig. 72. If material is loosely woven, place two rows of small machine stitches ⅛″ apart, and ⅛″ from raw edge. Fig. 73. Baste or pin near finish line, and catch-stitch hem to lining only, except at seams. Fig. 74. Because taut stitches break under strain, use loose stitches. Be sure they do not catch into the top of the skirt when it is lined, or they will show on the outside of the garment.

Plain Straight Hem

Completely finish dress, or skirt, before hemming. Mark the hem, using

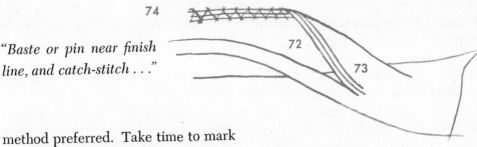

74

"Baste or pin near finish line, and catch-stitch . . ."

72

73

method preferred. Take time to mark accurately for best results.

Miter the skirt seam margins, narrow at end of seam but widened to normal width at crease of hem.

Place the garment on table and crease-baste at hem marks. Place a second row of bastings about 2″ above the crease basting, easing in fullness. Measure and trim hem 2½″ wide with pinking shears, if desired.

Press hem with up and down motion on wrong side of skirt, using a press cloth. Never press crosswise or the hem will be stretched out of shape. Trim lining at hem crease and catch-stitch with large stitches. When pressing raw edge of hem, slip a piece of heavy paper between hem and garment to keep edge from indenting on right side.

Machine stitch a scant ⅛″ or ¼″ from the raw edge of hem with small stitches.

Stitch two rows ⅛″ apart if material is sheer. If material is cotton, silk, or sheer wool, feather stitch hem by picking up one or two threads in dress or skirt; then alternate, catching in machine stitching of hem. Keep stitches at least ¼″ apart, and do not pull thread taut.

Blind Stitched Hem

This type of hem is used on very sheer, unlined garments, for sleeves and skirt hems.

Mark and press first hem turn. Allow an extra hem's width in *sheer skirts*. Turn up depth of hem desired, press, and lightly catch-stitch to crease. This prevents wrinkling of inner hem after wearing and laundering. Then turn up full width again. This avoids a shadow line of the seam allowance.

To finish hem, enter needle in crease of second hem turn. Take small stitches about ⅛″ apart, slipping the needle in the fold of the hem turn. Turn about ⅛″ and bring out needle to pick up a thread in the garment. Try to keep the stitches invisible on the right and wrong side, or the hem will not be "blind."

Plain Hem with Machine Stitched Edge

This hem is finished the same as the plain straight hem edge, except for the machine stitching.

Turn under ¼″ and machine stitch

close to the crease; then catch-stitch to the garment. This type of hem is preferred for cottons that are washed regularly and receive hard wear.

Underhemming is recommended for this type of hem in heavyweight or bulky fabrics, and other garments that will receive hard wear. (See Underhemming, page 51.)

Hems Trimmed with Rows of Stitching

Mark and baste accurately because decorated hems are unattractive unless evenly measured and stitched. Press thoroughly and shrink out fullness. Baste guide lines for accurate machine stitching. If the material is heavy, do not turn top edge of hem under. Leave the raw edge on and pink, or overcast, because the multiple stitching will prevent it from raveling.

Place as many rows of stitching as desired for the trim. This type of hem is recommended for circular, or flared, skirts. It is always wise to baste several times before stitching to keep material smooth when sewing by machine. Stitch next to guide basting, not on it. Start decorative stitching close to crease of hem and work up. Stitch from the right side, and in same direction in each row of stitching, to avoid bias wrinkling between rows.

Bound Hems in Unlined Garments

This hem is used extensively in men's tailoring, women's half-lined garments, and garments with zip-in linings. Bias binding made from lining fabric makes the most attractively finished garment. (See Bias Bindings, page 32.)

Bind the raw edge of the hem with bias binding by placing right side of binding and right side of hem together and stitching ⅛" from edge. Press and turn binding to inside of hem, and baste in place.

Crease hem binding and garment between thumb and forefinger and finish, using felling stitch.

Take small stitch in tape; then pick up one or two threads of the garment, keeping stitches about ⅛" apart. Fig. 75. Do not pull thread taut at any time. This is a very fast and easy stitch. It is the same as running basting, with the exception of stitching alternately into garment and binding until hem is completed.

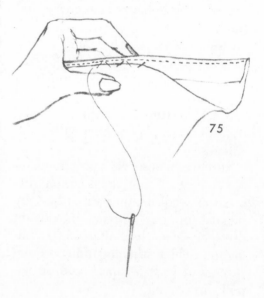

75

Faced Hem

This hem is used when lengthening, or remodeling garments.

Prepared hem binding is available in several different shades, or it may be made of a lightweight fabric. When making a garment longer, be sure the facing will finish where the hem crease formerly was. This helps to camouflage the alteration.

After hems have been in a garment any length of time, it is almost impossible to remove the hem crease entirely. Use a press cloth dampened with white vinegar water; then rub slightly with fine sandpaper on the hem crease to help erase the mark.

Join the facing to the hem with about a ¼″ seam. Press hem and facing open but do not stretch bottom of garment. Flat stitch all seam margins to facing, from right side.

Crease hem and facing between thumb and forefinger, with facing slightly rolled underneath, and baste. Trim the seam narrower on the inside of the hem. Press again and baste, or pin, the top in place. Using felling or catch-stitch, sew facing and garment together loosely.

Interfaced Hems

Use this type of hem for woolen garments that are not lined to hemline. When using an interfaced hem, match the interfacing with the garment material as closely as possible. Black may be used with *navy*. When the fabric is difficult to match, lining material may be used.

If the skirt is gored or circular, make the interfacing ½″ deeper than the hem, turn and cut on the bias. If the skirt is straight, it is best that the interfacing be cut on the same grain line as the garment. Measure hem, crease, baste, and press. Remove bastings.

Open hem, and place the interfacing over it, from crease to ½″ beyond raw edge.

Attach interfacing by catch-stitching by hand in the hem crease. Fig. 76. Then machine stitch close to raw edge of garment. Fig. 77. This raw edge may be permanently basted, instead of machine stitched. Place a row of small machine stitching ¼″ from extended edge of interfacing. Fig. 78. See page 52.

If desired, pink the garment close to the machine stitching and raw edge of extended interfacing.

Turn and baste, or pin, hem in position. Press; then crease between thumb and forefinger if material is heavy.

Pick up a small stitch in garment, then a small stitch in machine stitching of the interfacing next to the skirt, as done in bias-bound hems. Fig. 79, page 52.

If using lightweight material, feather stitch, as in plain hem, on top of the machine stitching of the extended interfacing.

Underhemming

When hemming heavy or bulky garments, underhemming provides

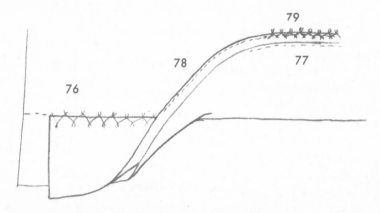

the most invisible finish. Prepare hem, as in previous instructions, by marking, crease-basting, and pressing. Trim hem turn, and machine stitch around the raw edge. Crease garment and hem turn between thumb and forefinger of left hand. (See Fig. 75, Bound Hems in Unlined Garments.) Take alternating stitches into machine stitching of hem turn and into garment. Do not pull stitches taut.

QUESTIONS

1. What type of thread is recommended for hems?
2. How can skirt lengths be determined? What should be worn when checking skirt lengths?
3. How do you hem lined skirts?
4. Where should hem be basted first for try-on?
5. How do you finish unlined hems of straight skirts?
6. What is blind stitching? When is it used?
7. How is a plain hem with machine stitched edge prepared? Where is it used?

8. In hems trimmed with rows of machine stitching, where do you begin machine stitching? Why?
9. On what type of garment is the bound hem most used?
10. When is the faced hem used?
11. Why are hems interfaced?
12. Describe how interfaced hems are constructed.
13. Describe underhemming.

Buttonholes

Bound Buttonhole

Baste a strip of organdy on the wrong side of material for buttonhole reinforcement. Draw a line on organdy at center front. Fig. 80-80.

A guide for marking buttonholes can be easily made. Using a 4½″ or 5″ square of sandpaper, draw a line ⅜″ from the edge on the smooth surface. Then mark off five rectangular slots of the most commonly used buttonhole sizes—¾″ x ¼″, 1″ x ¼″, 1⅛″ x ¼″, 1¼″ x ¼″, and 1⅜″ x ¼″. Each slot should be the same distance from the penciled line as its respective

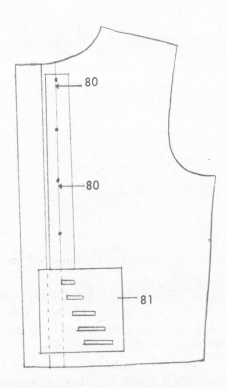

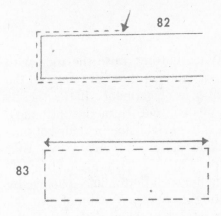

buttonholes larger than #60 are desired, simply slide the buttonhole guide toward the side seam of the garment. *Increase the size of buttonhole slightly for very thick buttons.*

Machine stitch, using small stitching, around penciled outline, starting in center of long side. Pivot on the needle to keep corners square. Fig. 82.

length. For example, see first slot, Fig. 81. Length from dotted line to dotted line equals the length of the slot.

Decide the distance between buttonhole spacing and size of the buttonhole to be made. The sandpaper buttonhole guide will insure accurately aligned buttonholes, finished the correct distance from finished edge of front.

Place sandpaper guide with rough side against fabric to keep it in place, on center front line, at buttonhole marks, and draw inside pattern with a sharp pencil. Fig. 81. The smallest slot is for a #24 or #28 size buttonhole and the largest is for a #60. If

Turn to the right side and baste a strip of garment material cut on the cross-grain of material, 1 inch wider than buttonhole width, with right sides of materials facing.

Turn back to wrong side and machine stitch from end to end, parallel to pattern stitching, but not across ends. Fig. 83. When using very sheer materials, fold ⅛″ tuck in center of boxing on right side and baste tuck inside box stitching before machine stitching, to insure wider seam allowance for finishing welts or bindings. Fig. 84. See page 54.

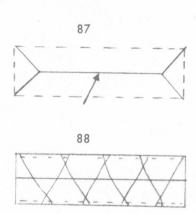

87

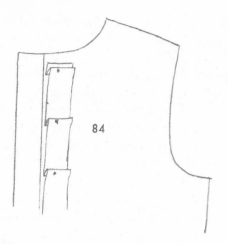

84

88

When cutting, raise the tuck with scissors and cut through center on the right side of garment. If the tuck is eliminated, cut through buttonhole strips from right side in center of buttonhole pattern to create two welt strips, Fig. 85. Trim welt strips 1″ wide between buttonhole spacings by cutting away excess material, Fig. 86. Separate welt strips with the finger tips and cut from the center of buttonhole to ⅛″ of each end through front and buttonhole interfacing, then diagonally to each corner. Be sure to

cut all the way to stitching but *not* through it. Fig. 87.

Turn welt strips to the wrong side and press raw edges, or seam margins, away from openings or back into the garment, then baste welts from the right side, equally divided, and catch-stitch firmly together. *Baste in welt or binding only,* Fig. 88. Turn to the wrong side and press welts to form equal tucks to the end of welts, Fig. 89.

Place under machine foot with narrow seam margin facing you and machine stitch directly on top, or slightly to left, of previous stitching, full length of pressed tuck, Fig. 90. Stitch through welt from the wrong side of

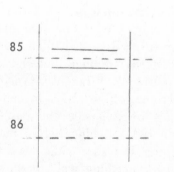

85

86

89

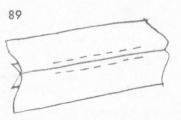

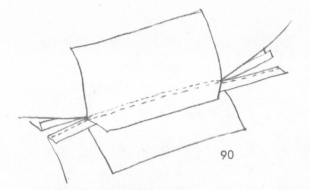

90

*"Stitch through welt from the
wrong side of garment, . . ."*

garment, with wider part of the welt facing machine feeder and narrow seam margin facing you.

Using sharp pointed scissors, poke V's out. Stitch across ends, just inside stitching of pattern boxing. These V's are very small. Fig. 91.

To finish inside of facing, baste around the buttonhole to keep the facing and garment together. Place a pin in each end and cut from the center to within ⅛" of buttonhole on garment facing, as in previous instructions. Tuck raw edges under and slip stitch lightly by hand (within welt only) so the buttonhole appears the same on the facing as on the outside of the garment.

When making buttonholes in sheer wool, cotton, or silk fabric, thread yarn, or string through a darning needle and back the eye through welts, or bindings, to act as a filler before stitching across the ends, Fig. 92.

If you are using organdy, or some similar fabric, for interfacing, shrink and baste to the wrong side of front carefully, then make buttonholes through the interfacing as in previous instructions. Do not make buttonholes through hair cloth or hymo interfacing. After the buttonholes are completed and wool interfacing is basted to garment, cut windows in interfacing, the size of buttonhole

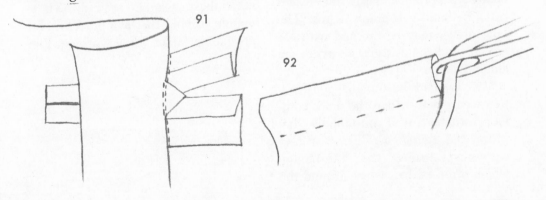

91

92

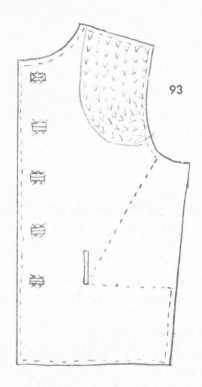

93

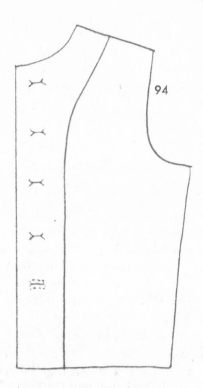

94

welts, and pull buttonhole seam allowance through. Catch-stitch to interfacing, Fig. 93.

Place a pin at each end of the buttonhole, through facing. Cut from center to ⅛″ from each pin and diagonally to corners. Turn under and catch by hand with fine stitches. The buttonholes may be finished with V's cut at ends and squared or in an almond shape, Fig. 94.

This type of buttonhole construction wears better than the more common, stitched welt buttonhole, because the seams are blended and cushioned against the interfacing, which protects the surface around the buttonhole from the wear of constant use.

Hand-Worked or Tailored Buttonholes

After the garment has been completed, baste a square around the buttonhole to hold the facing, front, and interfacing intact while working, Fig. 95.

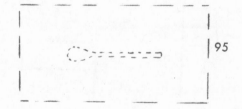

95

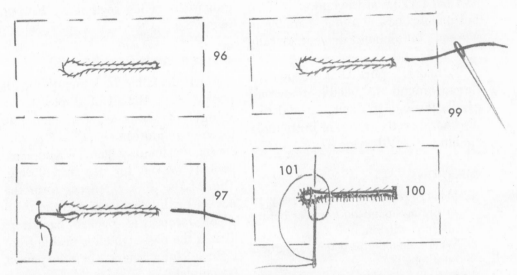

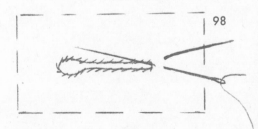

Machine stitch the outline of the buttonhole inside the square basting with small machine stitches in a keyhole design. Cut between the machine stitching and round out the curved end; overcast scant 1/16″ around the buttonhole opening, Fig. 96.

Thread a large needle with buttonhole gimp and run the needle between the facing and front, coming out at the inside end of the buttonhole. Leave the gimp thread extended at the end and long enough to rethread the needle. Pin gimp along buttonhole opening to hold in place before starting to work the buttonhole with purl stitches, using silk, or linen buttonhole thread, Fig. 97.

Slip the needle between the front and facing about 1″ from end of buttonhole to keep the ends from sticking out when they are clipped. Work buttonhole, using purl stitch, with rayon or silk floss, keeping the purl knots exactly on top of the buttonhole opening. Be careful not to get the stitches too close together or the buttonhole will buckle and stand open when finished, Fig. 98.

Rethread extended gimp after you have worked all around the buttonhole opening; then work needle with gimp between front and facing before clipping away the gimp thread, Fig. 99.

After you have worked around the buttonhole with purl knot, bar tack the inside end for strength, Fig. 100.

The bar tacking at the end of worked buttonhole may continue parallel to worked buttonhole or horizontally across the end.

To make a purl knot, throw the thread around the needle, then pull needle through the material and rest the knot directly on top of buttonhole opening, Fig. 101, page 57.

QUESTIONS

1. What three steps are necessary in preparing bound buttonholes before machine stitching?
2. Where should the penciled pattern be stitched?
3. Describe the three steps which follow stitching of the penciled pattern.
4. Which way should buttonhole seam margins be pressed?
5. Describe the completion of a bound buttonhole.
6. How are corded buttonholes constructed?
7. When should buttonhole strips be interfaced with organdy?
8. At what stage are hand-tailored buttonholes placed in a garment?
9. What is the function of gimp thread?
10. Describe the stitches used in hand-tailored buttonholes.

Pocket Construction

The following group of pocket instructions may be adapted to various types of pockets, including flap pockets, patch pockets, stitched, or unfinished welts. The measurements given are taken from standard pocket measurements and should be graded slightly according to the size of the

individual. (See section on Fitting, page 73.)

Double Welt Pocket

Mark or tailor tack mouthline of pocket, Fig. 102. Cut 3 pieces, on straight of goods, 3″ x 7″ and one piece of reinforcement 4″ x 8″, using silesia, muslin, or wigan. Wigan is especially woven for use in tailoring. Two of the 3″ x 7″ pieces form the pocket binding, or welt, and the third piece forms the pocket backdrop. This is the piece which is visible from right side of garment when the pocket is complete.

Baste reinforcement material in center of mouthline on wrong side of garment, Fig. 103.

Turn to right side and baste 2 strips, 3″ x 7″, butted together, on the chalk line, right sides of the material facing the right side of garment. Baste and machine stitch a scant ¼″ from the chalk line and tack, or tie, stitches, Fig. 104. When using sheer material, stitch pocket binding ⅛″ from chalk mark.

102

103

104

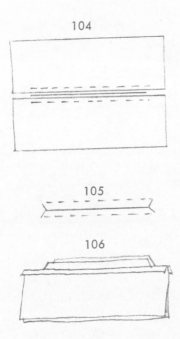

105

106

108

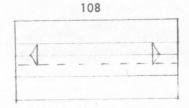

109

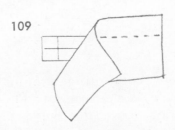

Slash on the wrong side, through garment, from center to within ¼″ of each end. Cut V-shape corners to machine stitching, Fig. 105. Turn welt to the wrong side and press seams open, Fig. 106.

Baste welts a scant ¼″ or ⅛″ wide, in welts only, and catch-stitch together from the right side, Fig. 107.

Take the third 3″ x 7″ piece and place about ½″ above upper pocket welt on the wrong side. Turn to the right side and baste in welt only, Fig. 109.

Top-stitch between the welt and garment seam if fabric is very heavy, or stitch from the wrong side in the same stitching as on lower welt. If machine will not take heavy seams, hand-stitch from the right side of garment between welt and garment, using backstitch, with heavy-duty thread, Fig. 110.

Sew silk pocket pieces to facing and backdrop of garment fabric. Press seam flat, *not open*. Pull V's through and stitch as close to the garment as

107

Turn to wrong side, press the seams open on a seam board all the way to ends, and machine stitch in the same stitching as in previous operation on lower welt, Fig. 108.

110

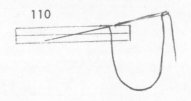

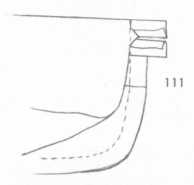

111

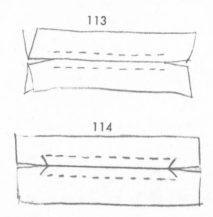

113

114

possible, continuing around the pocket to close permanently, Fig. 111.

Always curve the bottom of a pocket. Do not square pockets, because corners are lint collectors. Clip pocket welts where V's are stitched by machine so they will lie flat. When using a sheer fabric, cut pocket and backdrop as one unit, Fig. 112.

Bound Pocket with Single Welt

Mark same as for a bound buttonhole pocket and baste reinforcement on the wrong side. Baste the two welts butted against chalk mark as in a double welt pocket, Fig. 113.

112

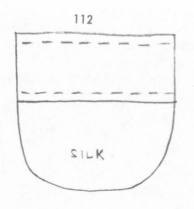

SILK

Machine stitch and cut from the wrong side. *Remember:* The width between the rows of machine stitching will be the width of the finished welt, Fig. 114.

Press seam open and baste lower welt the full width between two rows of stitches of pocket mouthline instead of two narrow welts.

Catch-stitch welt shut and press on the wrong side all the way to the ends of welts, Fig. 115. Press the upper welt open, then back together. Machine stitch lower welt in first stitching on wrong side, Fig. 116. When using this type of pocket on men's clothing, top stitch on the right side for strength, where backdrop is joined to the pocket.

Pull V's through and stitch pocket piece to back-up piece (top welt) and facing, as in buttonhole pocket. Don't press seam open where pocket pieces

115

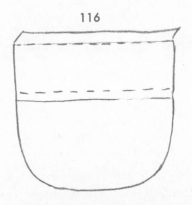

116

and backdrop are joined together to complete pocket.

Angle Pocket with Flap

Cut the interlining the same shape as flap, minus seam margin, and catch-stitch to flap, Fig. 117. Ease wool flap onto silk lining piece and press out fullness before machine stitching. Machine stitch flap and lining together around edge of interfacing on stitching line. Then trim curves to ⅛″ and turn to right side.

Edge-baste curved edge and overcast top raw edges of flap before pressing to keep the lining from showing. Fig. 118.

117

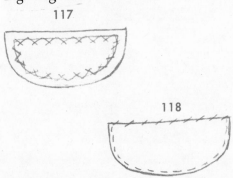

118

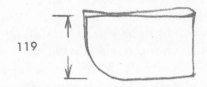

119

Fold ends of flap together, and measuring from the bottom to seam allowance, mark both ends of flap. This assures equal width across flap, Fig. 119.

Baste flap, overlapping chalk line ¼″ or required seam allowance, right sides facing garment, Fig. 120.

Lift up seam of flap and slip 3″ x 7″ welt piece under seam, raw edge butted against stitching, Fig. 121.

Machine stitch on chalk line across flap, stopping where flap ends. Use angle of flap as a guide for stitching, Fig. 122.

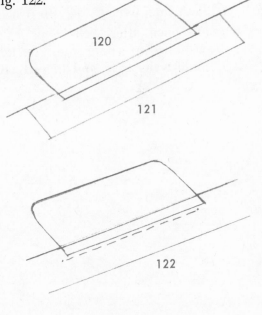

120

121

122

Fold seam margin of flap back and finish as a single welt pocket. When cutting to form V's, be careful *not* to cut too far or angle flap will not conceal lower welt. *Note:* If you cut too far at each corner, you will have to remove the flap and make a larger one to cover the opening. Finish as a single welt pocket.

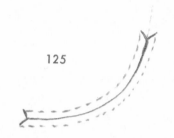

125

Curved Buttonhole Pocket

Draw outline of the pocket on right side of garment in proper position, according to individual taste. Baste reinforcement on wrong side, completely covering pocket curve, Fig. 123.

Baste 1½″ bias strips butted together about ⅛″ from chalk mark. Machine stitch just outside basting line, finishing evenly at each end, Fig. 124.

Slash from wrong side. Press both seams open after welt strips have been turned to wrong side, Fig. 125.

Baste welts from end to end. Be sure bastings are *in welt only*, close to stitching line. Catch-stitch welts together, stitching all the way through. Machine stitch lower welt from the wrong side in previous machine stitching, as in bound buttonhole, Fig. 126.

Cut pocket pieces and pocket backing according to curve of pocket opening. Cut lower pocket piece of lining material. Fig. 127.

Join the lining to raw edges of lower pocket welt. Fig. 128.

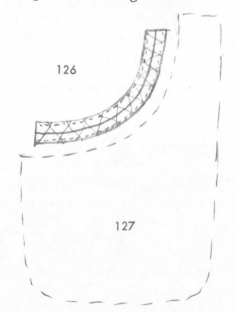

126

127

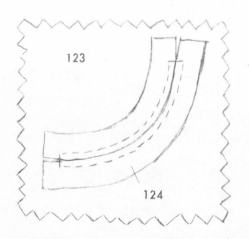

123

124

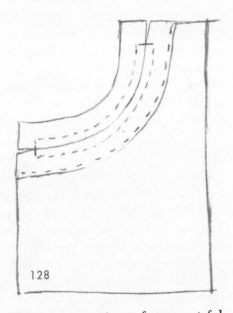

128

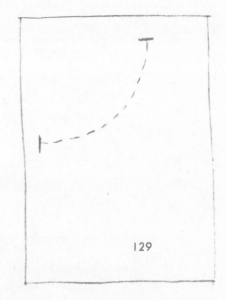

129

Cut a square piece of garment fabric, large enough to cover mouthline, to form pocket backdrop. Baste just above upper pocket welt and machine stitch from right or wrong side of garment, depending on the angle of the curve, or backstitch by hand, between garment and upper welt. This attaches the pocket piece that has been basted in place previously, from the right side of the garment, Fig. 129.

Pull V's through and close the same as for buttonhole welts. Close pocket on the wrong side by joining pocket sections as in previous pocket instructions. Blend seams by trimming away excess material, Fig. 130.

Finish ends of pocket with hand-worked arrows. Refer to instructions for Arrow-head and Crow's-foot Trim, pages 64 and 65.

Double Curved Pocket

When making a curved pocket with a rolling curve, use one large piece of material with nap and grain-line running parallel to nap and grain-line of material.

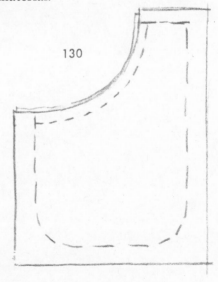

130

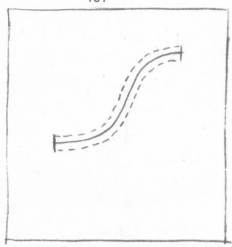

131

Baste reinforcement in back of the pocket outline. Machine stitch to each end, but *not across end*. Tighten stitches firmly, Fig. 131.

Slash from center to each end, cutting V's in material but *not* in pocket welts, Fig. 132.

Slash through the pocket welt piece from the end of pocket opening to outer edge so as to give you two welt pieces instead of the one piece you started with, Fig. 133.

To complete pocket, refer to instructions for Curved Welt Pocket, page 62.

Arrow-heads

The widths of the welts will form the base of the arrow. The height should equal the length of the base. Using silk buttonhole twist, enter needle at right corner of welt and draw through at left corner, Fig. 134. To make outline of arrow, pick up thread of fabric at top, Fig. 135. Then insert needle in lower right corner: Continue stitching, dropping down a

132

133

134

135

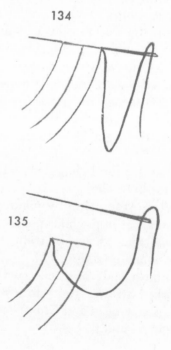

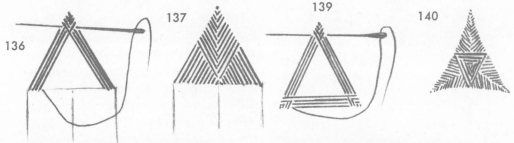

stitch each time at the top, and moving inside at the bottom, Fig. 136, until the arrow is completely filled in, Fig. 137.

Arrow-heads strengthen pockets and add a professional touch. They may be used for trim on darts, buttonholes, and pleats, depending on the style of the garment.

Crow's-foot Tacks

Crow's-foot tacks are similar to arrow-heads. Draw an outline with a basting thread or chalk, and curve the bottom slightly, Fig. 138. Start work-

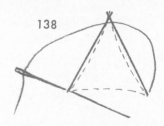

ing from the left-hand corner and continue as in arrow-heads except, work from corner to corner, picking up stitches outside the outline, Fig. 139. Continue until completely filled in, Fig. 140.

Overcoat Welt Pocket

Make a welt pattern of desired angle with long sides measuring 7″. Place pattern on fold of the fabric and cut welt as shown, Fig. 141.

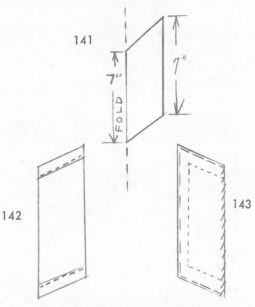

Catch-stitch welt interlining of wigan to welt. Fold in half, right sides facing, stitching ends together, using ½″ seam, Fig. 142. Turn and edge-baste. Press and top-stitch ½″ on three sides, when using machine stitching. Overcast raw edges ⅛″, Fig. 143. Measure ends of welt to assure equal

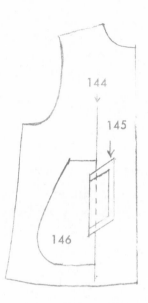

144

145

146

width. (See Angle pocket with Flap, Fig. 119, page 61.)

When using interfacing in a pocket welt with hand-picked or saddle-stitched trim, cut interfacing from folded welt pattern, minus seam allowance at each end. Baste interfacing in the pocket welt until machine stitched, or hand stitched. (See Saddle-stitch instructions, page 29.)

On the right side of garment, draw

a chalk mark on the mouthline of garment longer than the pocket welt, Fig. 144. Baste reinforcement on the wrong side in center of mouthline, completely covering the pocket opening. Baste flap, or welt, on line for pocket opening, overlapping ⅜″. Machine stitch and tack, Fig. 145. Note the angle corners. Baste under pocket piece on the opposite side of welt, slipped under welt seam margin, butted against stitching of welt, or flap, Fig. 146.

Machine stitch pocket piece opposite the welt, parallel to the raw edge. Do not have machine stitchings more than ½″ apart, where welt and pocket piece are attached to the garment. Tack or tie stitch at each end.

Note: Stop the pocket piece stitching a little short of welt stitching so the V's will be covered by welts when finished, Fig. 147.

Slash from center to ends and press pocket piece seam open, then press *back* together, Fig. 148. Turn welt seam to the wrong side and baste upper pocket piece to welt seam with

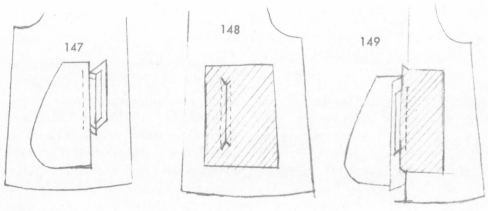

147

148

149

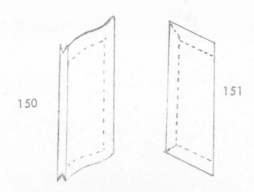

150

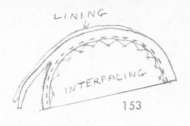

151

upper pocket piece of silk to eliminate bulk. Fell the ends of welts by hand. Reinforce on wrong side of garment with diagonal basting. If working with heavy wools, make both pocket pieces of silk, silesia, or wigan material.

Overcoat Patch Pocket or Sneak Pocket

Cut flap and lining the same size. Ease wool flap and lining together, keeping wool on top when basting. Press and shrink fullness before stitching. Machine stitch ¼″ from edge; trim curves to ⅛″, Fig. 153. Turn

right sides together. Machine stitch in same stitching that holds welt to garment, Fig. 149. Turn to *right* side on men's or boys' coats; baste and top stitch welt for strength where welt, or flap, and pocket are joined. Leave V's on right side of coat and catch-stitch onto under pocket piece, Fig. 150. Baste welt, or flap, to garment and stitch across ends of welts stitching where connected to coat, and back across ends of welt to strengthen pocket, Fig. 151.

Join pockets on wrong side, clipping corners where necessary, Fig. 152. If using medium wool make one

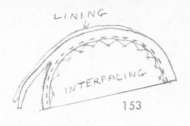

LINING

INTERFACING

153

154

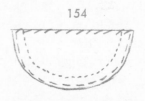

and edge baste; overcast raw edges, and press. Top stitch ½″ from edge of flap, Fig. 154. When using interfacing for flaps, cut the seam margin away and baste into place until top stitched to hold permanently, Fig. 153.

Cut patch pocket and lining the same size. Sew reinforcement tape to

152

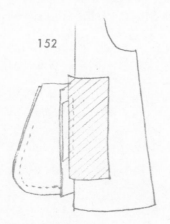

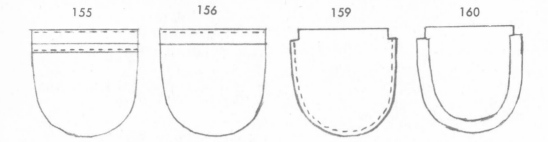

155   156   159   160

the pocket at crease of hem, stitching by machine on lower edge of tape, Fig. 155.

Sew bias binding, or lining, to raw edge of the pocket patch, with right sides of tape, or lining, facing the right side of pocket. Crease hem of pocket where tape has been stitched, and press, Fig. 156. Fold at crease of pocket hem, right sides facing. Stitch ends of hem at sides, Fig. 157. Trim lining the same length as the pocket.

In an unlined pocket, turn the bias binding under and top stitch. Slip stitch to pocket. Clip in at lower edge of side hem, Fig. 158. Press and machine stitch close to edge around pocket, Fig. 159.

Draw, or tailor tack, outline of pocket where it is to be sewn on the garment; remove patch and draw second line ¾″ inside first outline, Fig. 160. Reduce the width of the inside line to ⅝″ or ½″ when making smaller pockets.

Lay pockets on the outline, right side up, and make sewing guide marks across pocket and garment, Fig. 161. Remove patch and extend marks past the second drawn line on garment, underneath pocket patch, Fig. 162. Fold patch pocket in half and notch the center bottom, corners, and center of sides before sewing, matching guide marks.

Trim edge of pocket to a scant ¼″ seam. Butt raw seam allowance against inside line, matching guide lines. Stitch, easing fullness of pocket

161   162

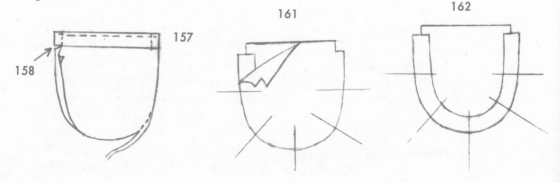

157

158

68

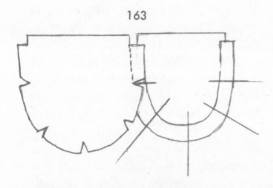

163

166   167

around curve, keeping *lines* and *notches* matched, Fig. 163.

Hold garment *firmly* and pocket patch *loosely* while sewing. When stopping the machine, be sure the needle is in the material to keep pocket and garment fabric in place.

Press on wrong side of garment and top stitch by machine ½″ from the edge on right side, starting at the inside seam, sewing toward corner. Backstitch for strength, Fig. 164. When finishing this type of pocket by hand, and eliminating top stitching, baste around the pocket where top stitching would have been. Turn pocket inside out and fell lining to

165

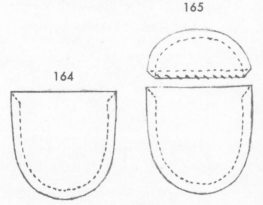

164

garment along basting. Keep stitches fairly close together to seal the raw seam between the lining and the garment.

Measure ends of flap to assure equal width. (See Angle Pocket with Flap, page 61, Fig. 119.) Set pocket flap about ⅜″ above patch, right sides facing. Baste and machine stitch ¼″ from the raw edge, stopping at very edge of flap. Clip away corners of flap, Fig. 165. Press down and machine stitch ½″ on right side. Tack, or tie, threads, Fig. 166. Keep top stitching on pocket and flap the same width. Make sure the flap covers the top of pocket patch on each side. Saddle-stitching or hand-picking adds a decorative trim.

Hand-Finished Patch Pocket

Follow instructions on commercial pattern. When using jersey or loosely woven fabric, cut organdy or wigan interfacing, the same shape as the pocket, minus seam allowance. Catch-stitch to wrong side of top pocket piece before attaching lining. With

69

right sides facing, keep top pocket piece on top of lining, over-finger as you baste and ease the two pieces together. This eases fullness in the top section onto lining and conceals lining when finished.

Machine stitch around pocket and lining, cutting across corners with two or three stitches, leaving about a 2″ opening, preferably at the bottom of pocket. Blend seams before turning and pressing. It is always best to edge baste before pressing.

Baste pocket to garment, close to edge of pocket. Stitch diagonally around pocket, from wrong side of garment, with waxed thread. Tack corner firmly, with two or three cross-stitches, and back-stitch to form a cross-stitch around the pocket, Fig. 167, page 69.

Breast Pocket

Cut a welt from pattern 1½″ wide and 4½″ long, making sure the sides of welt are cut on the grain-line of fabric. Crease baste ¼″ seam on edge of the welt, and press. Cut lining of wigan, or organdy, same as welt, minus ¼″ seam.

Catch-stitch interlining at crease of welt, making sure stitches are invisible on right side. Clip corners of welt to reduce bulk, Fig. 168. Catch-stitch raw edge of welt to interfacing, Fig. 169. After pressing edges to razor sharpness, turn to right side and machine stitch on edge of welt, or saddle-stitch by hand. Omit machine or saddle-stitch if finishing by hand.

Measure ends of welt to assure equal width. (See Angle Pocket with Flap, Fig. 119, page 61.) Be sure chalk mark mouthline on garment extends beyond ends of welt. Baste flap ¼″, over-lapping mouthline, and machine stitch on chalk mark, Fig. 170.

Cut pocket lining like welt pattern; extend lining material about 8″ longer and ½″ wider, cutting lower end of lining on an angle. Clip corner ⅛″, as shown in Fig. 171.

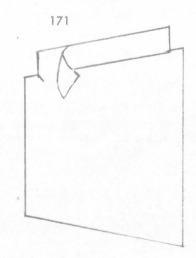

171

168

169

170

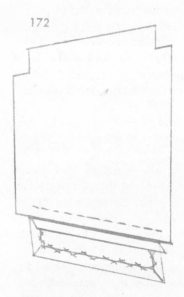

172

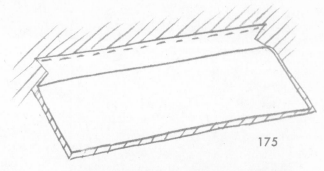

175

Flat stitch upper edge of pocket lining to garment on right side to make pocket stronger. The welt will cover this stitching, Fig. 173. Tack V's flat on top of under pocket lining, Fig. 174. *Note:* Do not pull V's through and machine stitch.

Pull lining up and baste welt piece of lining, with raw seams turned under, to pocket welt; slip stitch a little short of welt edge inside of welt, Fig. 175.

Backstitch by hand in stitching between welt and garment, or machine stitch from right side, whichever is preferred, so stitches are invisible, Fig. 176.

Baste welts on top of V's at each

Ease lining edge under welt seam margin, and baste. Machine stitch ¼″ from edge, stopping a little short at each end so stitching does not extend beyond welt, Fig. 172.

Slash from the wrong side, between two rows of stitching, from center to ¼″ from each end, and diagonally to stitching, leaving V's about ¼″ long. *Be careful not to cut welt.* Pull pocket lining to inside of garment. Press welt and garment edges open.

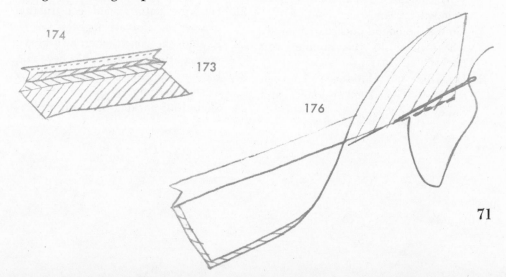

174

173

176

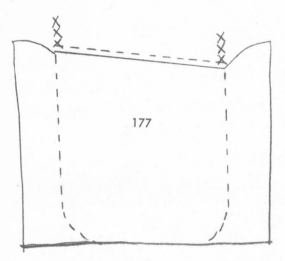

177

end and fell welt by hand on right side. Pull needle through to wrong side and tack firmly with diagonal stitching. Turn to wrong side and close pocket by machine stitching each side, rounding the bottom corners, Fig. 177. Blend seams.

QUESTIONS

1. How is a pocket size determined?
2. Describe a double welt pocket.
3. When is it necessary to top stitch the double welt pocket?
4. Why should pocket linings have rounded corners?
5. How is the bound pocket with single welt similar to the double welt pocket?
6. Describe the difference between single welt pockets on men's and ladies' garments.
7. Describe the construction of pocket flaps.
8. Why is caution necessary when cutting V's between welt and flap in angle pockets?
9. Describe the construction of a curved pocket.
10. What kind of fabric should be used for pocket backdrop in curved pockets?
11. Compare the welts of the double curve pocket and the curved pocket.
12. Describe the construction of an arrow-head.
13. How do crow's-foot tacks differ from arrow-heads?
14. How are overcoat pocket welts finished and placed on garment?
15. What caution is necessary in cutting V's of overcoat welt pocket?
16. How should V's and pocket welts be finished?
17. Explain construction and placement of flap in the overcoat patch, or sneak pocket.
18. Explain preparation and construction of sneak pocket.
19. Explain the difference between lined and unlined sneak pocket.
20. How does the hand-finished patch pocket differ from the machine stitched pocket?
21. Describe pattern and construction of welt for a breast pocket.
22. Explain the construction of a breast pocket after mouthline has been cut.
23. Explain the attaching of the lining of a breast pocket.
24. Should all pockets be reinforced?

3. Preparation for Garment Construction

Various Figure Types

There is no "perfect figure" or the "perfect 36." Heredity, living habits, illness, accidents and many other factors affect our physical structure and appearance. All figures change with age, bone structure settles and the body becomes shorter and more prone to become fat.

Proper rest, diet, and exercise can help to counteract some figure problems, but those which cannot be helped can be minimized by careful fitting and altering of tailored garments.

Let your guide be, "My personal appearance is my best salesman." Study your reflection from all angles in a full-length mirror, and encourage criticism and suggestions from family and friends; let this information guide you in choosing your wardrobe.

Following are some of the most common figure types and suggested pattern alterations which are necessary for smooth-fitting garments.

In the "normal," or "average" figure, the shoulders are usually square; head and neck are held erect; the waist is 10 inches smaller than the hips; and the height is about five feet six inches. This individual will have very few style and fitting problems. Regardless of figure type, patterns should be purchased by bust measurement.

The larger figure, with round shoulders, is accompanied by a large and sagging bustline, Fig. 178. Patterns do not cope with these problems, so this person will have to alter the pattern before cutting. First, slash the pattern through waist dart to ⅛″ from shoulder. Slash side dart to ⅛″ of slash line and spread both slashes according to the amount needed for bust measurement, Fig. 179, page 74.

If the abdomen is oversized, slash through waist dart to crest of bust and diagonally to ⅛″ from armscye, Fig. 180. Spread pattern the amount needed. Do the same with the skirt front, slashing from waist toward hemline, and in the garment, forming unpressed pleats, darts, or gathers from this added ease. See page 74.

A fraction should be added to the shoulder and neck seam in the back, depending upon how stooped the shoulders are, Fig. 181, page 74.

Stitch the shoulder dart deeper and

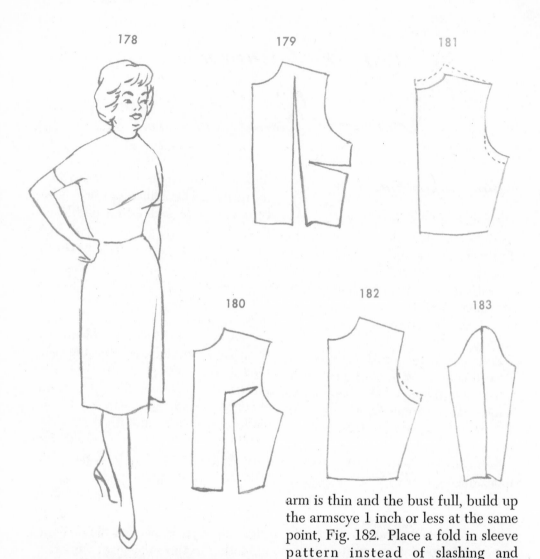

178

179

181

180

182

183

longer in front to meet the crest of the bust. If there is an underarm dart, drop it down until it points to the crest of the bustline. If the upper arm is full, cut the armscye 1 inch or less, and deeper at the side seam. Slash pattern from center top of sleeve toward elbow, or as far as necessary. Spread pattern 1 inch or less. If the arm is thin and the bust full, build up the armscye 1 inch or less at the same point, Fig. 182. Place a fold in sleeve pattern instead of slashing and spreading, Fig. 183.

A person with a long neck and sloping shoulders has the most common fitting problem, Fig. 184. This can be corrected by stitching deeper on the shoulder seam at the armscye, gradually sloping into the regular seam about 1½" from the neck. Fig. 185. High, round neck styles with slightly

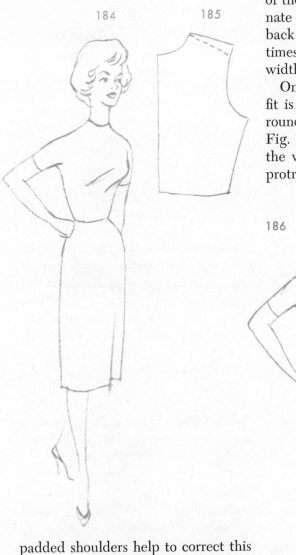

184   185

of the pattern must be raised to eliminate wrinkles or bulges across the back of the garment, Fig. 187. Sometimes it is necessary to increase the width across the shoulder.

One of the most difficult figures to fit is the person whose shoulders are round and head and neck tilt forward, Fig. 188. The small of the back, at the waist, sinks in and the abdomen protrudes. Place a tuck in the front of

186

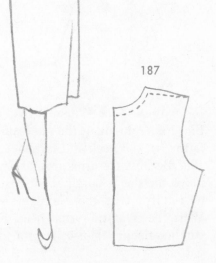

187

padded shoulders help to correct this figure problem. In extreme cases, it may be necessary to build up the neckline slightly in front and back.

The square shouldered type of person has an athletic appearance. Fig. 186. Tailored or casual clothes belong to this figure, with tweeds and worsteds being most suitable. The back

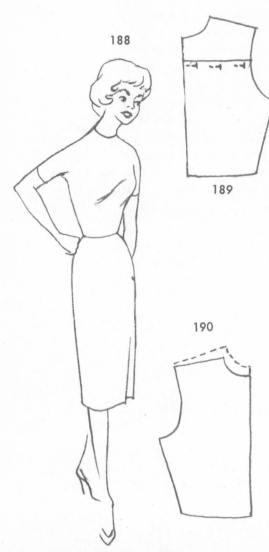

188

189

190

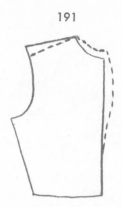

191

Make an accurately fitted muslin form for this type of figure, then fit your pattern pieces to the form before cutting the material. The form pieces can be transferred to heavy brown paper and used as a basic pattern from which commercial patterns can easily be adjusted.

When an individual has hump shoulders (most common in older people) it is best to use a pattern with a seam up the back, and cut as shown in Fig. 191.

QUESTIONS

1. What factors aid you in choosing proper styles?
2. What is the most difficult fitting problem of the larger figure? Should a pattern be altered in more than one place?
3. What do you do when the bust is full and arms thin?
4. What type of garment looks best on the athletic figure?
5. Which fitting problem is most common?

the pattern ¼″ or ½″ across the chest, Fig. 189. Add about the same amount to the back at neck and shoulder, Fig. 190. Because the arms swing forward, move the sleeve notch about ½″ or ¾″ to the front at the shoulder seam. Waist darts at the back need to be stitched deeper than called for in the pattern.

76

6. What type of figure is most difficult to fit?
7. What method is used when it is impossible to fit the pattern to a figure?

Choosing Styles

The selection of a pattern which complements the figure is very important. Here are some pointers which should be helpful in choosing a pattern.

The Tall, Stout Figure

• Choose a design with a V-neck.
• Medium length, double-breasted jacket is good. Jacket should never stop at widest part of hips.
• Simple, well tailored lines are best.
• Lapels should point slightly upward, giving the figure a streamlined appearance.
• A softly rolled collar and lapel are flattering.
• Vertical lines always appear slenderizing; hence, four-gore and six-gore skirts.

The Tall, Slender Figure

• Most attractive in suits.
• To reduce the appearance of height, use scalloped panels, fitted belts in contrasting colors and various widths, large patch pockets, or pockets with unusual flaps.
• Suits with yokes or belted waistlines are good.
• Choose wider or cuffed sleeves, to reduce appearance of arm length.

• Full, flared, or pleated skirts are most flattering.
• Full skirts tend to lead the gaze from the length of the legs.
• Fullness in one spot will make the figure look fuller at that point.

The Short, Stout Figure

• Choice of styles is limited.
• Short jacket is very good, preferably one with elongated lapels and a single waistline button.
• Width at the top will make hips appear smaller.
• A modified double-breasted jacket is becoming.
• Choose designs that run vertically, the length of the figure, to look taller.

The Short, Slender Figure

• Short jackets, ending slightly below the waist, are best.
• A longer skirt is becoming; it gives an illusion of height.
• Should stay away from ornate, highly decorative styles.
• Semi-fitted and set-in sleeves, with a short shoulder seam, tend to slenderize.

QUESTION

1. Describe the most suitable styles and fabrics for the four basic figure types.

Fabric Measurements

There are standard widths for different types of fabrics. Hand-loomed or homespun woolens, domestic or imported, come 27" to 30" wide. French woolens are usually 52" wide. Other woolens run 52" to 62" wide. These are mill-spun, domestic or imported. Check labels for origin of woolens and ask the dealer if woolens have been needle-shrunk.

Linens and cottons come approximately 36" to 39" wide. Linens should always be shrunk, and since they improve with laundering, there is no problem involved.

Cottons have a minimum of shrinkage. However, even sanforized cottons will shrink from 1 to 3 percent.

Silks average from 36" to 42" wide. They should be shrunk, using a steam-iron.

Synthetics range from 39" to 48" wide and should be treated like silk, unless guaranteed washable.

Before buying material, always check the amount of yardage required. It is much better to have a half yard too much than a half yard too little. Buy lining, foundation interfacing material, and all necessary trimmings at one time, to expedite the work. Since lining fabrics run narrow, purchase the same yardage as the garment fabric for a coat or suit jacket. Interfacing material should be purchased as long as finished length of garment. Always buy large spools of thread since more is required in tailoring than in ordinary sewing.

The following are some examples showing the amounts of material required for different garments. These figures are compiled for the average figure:

5 feet 6", size 36
 Suit, simple design and fabric— 3 yards
 Coat, plain—3½ yards
 Plain skirt—1⅛ yards

Plaids and checks should be matched in all directions to give a smart, well-groomed look. This requires more fabric. When buying checks, plaids, or material with a nap, check the pattern for reference to nap yardage. If no reference is given, buy one-half to one yard extra, especially if the material is a large plaid. Corduroy, velvet, gabardine, duvetyn and flannels have a nap. Many silks, cottons and other fabrics, too, have naps and must be purchased with this fact in mind.

QUESTIONS

1. How wide is homespun wool material?
2. Is it necessary to shrink all material?
3. When is it necessary to buy more material than called for in the pattern?

Shrinking Woolens

This is one of the most important steps in the making of a garment. It isn't advisable to make a garment and hope that the material will not shrink.

The material leaves the mill in rolls. Fabric brokerage houses, and some stores, unroll the material and fold it in half with right sides inside and roll it on to bolts. In doing this the inside fold of the woolen usually stretches out of grain-line.

Most sales personnel cut woolens by the design if there is one. If not, they try to cut it straight across the grain, which is not a true cut with the woof or cross thread. If the woolen is torn, the ends are true.

Before shrinking wool, check for the true cut of fabric. To do this, tear a small strip off each end to make it even, or pull a woof thread and cut on this line if the material will not tear. Pin the selvedge sides together to keep it in place. Snip into the selvedge about 12″ apart so it will lie smooth. If the fold of material appears warped and wrinkled, have someone help you gently stretch it before shrinking.

If you shrink material at home, use the London Shrunk Method:
- Spread newspapers on a flat surface. Place a dampened sheet, which has had the excess moisture removed, over them.
- Place the folded wool on half the sheet. Fold other half of the sheet over folded wool. If wool is longer than sheet, fold wool back over damp sheet.
- Fold wool and sheet together every 12″. Be careful not to wrinkle.
- Let stand until the wool absorbs the sheet's moisture, preferably overnight. Cover top layer with heavy paper, or plastic, to keep the moisture in.
- Unroll carefully and smooth out.
- Allow to dry at room temperature.
- Do not stretch while the material is damp.
- Press out wrinkles with iron set for a temperature to be used on wool, and while material is still damp. Sheet used for shrinking may be used for press cloth.

This is a "tried and true" method for shrinking wool, and is the best method for most people. Remember to allow about 3 inches per yard for normal shrinkage when buying wool that is not needle-shrunk. Handling wool carefully while shrinking will expedite the work in preparing it for the needle ("needle"-shrunk).

If this method seems to be too involved, and time is an important factor, perhaps your neighborhood cleaner or tailor will shrink the material. Reliable merchants do shrinking in the store before delivering merchandise to the customer.

Factory shrinking is not the same as needle shrinking. Wool shrinks after it leaves the factory, through steam pressing, atmospheric dampness, and body moisture. Therefore, it is important to shrink wool or see that it is needle shrunk before constructing a garment.

QUESTIONS

1. How do you prepare woolens for shrinking?
2. How much yardage is lost in shrinking?

4. Garment Construction

Unless a garment is made to fit accurately, it will be uncomfortable, unattractive and a waste of time and material. Persistent fitting of each section during construction is the secret of fine tailoring. Every operation is an integral part of an expertly tailored garment, although collars, sleeves and shoulder pads are the most difficult operations.

Shoulders should mold smoothly from the neck to the top of the sleeves. Fashion trends govern the size of shoulder pads and width of shoulders. The garment should drape straight from the shoulders to the hemline, without bulges and wrinkles. Sleeves should swing forward across the sides of the pockets, without bias wrinkles or pleats at armscye. Men's tailored garments should fit more snugly around the neck than should ladies' garments, with the shirt collar barely showing.

The armholes should be large enough for comfort but not so large that the garment rides up every time the arms are raised. Most people have different arm lengths, so be sure each sleeve is the correct length. Men's shirt sleeves may extend ½″ longer than finished sleeves and be in good taste.

Choosing a fitted or pleated trouser style is a matter of individual preference. Regardless of style, trousers must fit snugly around the waist so they stay up and fit smoothly across the hips. To insure room for comfort and action, it is best to sit down and walk around when being fitted for trousers. The upper part of the trouser leg is fitted according to leg size. The width of the trouser bottom is governed by the size of shoe worn— a little more than three-fourths the length of the shoe—unless the trousers are tapered. Wider trouser legs appear to reduce larger shoe sizes. Men's trousers should have a slight break over the top of the shoes, when finished.

The fitting of ladies' skirts and slacks is much the same as men's slacks except that skirt lengths are determined individually. Slacks should be somewhat more tapered and shorter than men's, unless fashion dictates otherwise.

A tailored garment is worth the cost and effort of making a foundation, which is the life structure of a garment, helping to retain the shape and permanent finish characteristic of fine tailoring. Foundation material can be purchased in different weights and combinations of fibers, such as wool, hair, and cotton blends. Linens, cottons and combinations are used in some wool and synthetic blended garments. A foundation of wool and hair fibers is usually best for woolen garments. Combinations of wool, hair, cotton, or linen fibers, also make suitable foundation fabrics for softly draped garments. Organdy, or nurses cloth, makes satisfactory foundations for washable garments, silks, and sheers. There are several new and blended synthetic materials available, but they should be individually tested for ability to withstand laundering and pressing, before being used.

Fitting the Pattern

Check the body measurements with a tape measure and compare with the pattern. Study the pattern and pin darts in all sections; pin all sections together and fit on the figure. Pin sleeve sections together, but do not pin the body section of the pattern.

If no one is available to help fit the pattern, lay it on a table, matching seam lines, and compare body measurements with the pattern measurements. Add or take away the amount where needed. *Note:* Never add or take away in one section. Add a small amount to each seam unless the abdomen or bust is large. If this is the case, check figure in the mirror and see if adjustments in bust, hips, or abdomen are necessary. Check the upper arm for pattern adjustment.

If you are using a three button suit pattern, be sure the top button is slightly above the crest of the bust, and the lower button ½" to ¾" below the natural waistline.

After the pattern pieces have been pinned together, fit them to the body, before cutting the material. Center the front and back of pattern sections to the spine and center front. This is not an accurate fitting but a close summary. If there are figure faults, make a muslin body pattern, complete with sleeves. For accurate fitting try on this pattern with shoulder pads in place. Rip apart and fit paper pattern to muslin pattern before cutting into material. Place pattern alterations according to muslin body pattern.

Placing of Darts

Darts are placed so the garment will fit the contours of the body; therefore, place them where they should be on the individual figure rather than following the pattern.

- Waist darts should end below the crest of the bust.
- Side darts should point toward the crest of the bust—not above or below it.
- Waist darts and fullness should be directly below the crest of the bust.

Skirt Darts

Skirt darts allow the skirt to fit the contours of the body, and to drape on the grain-line. Darts should point to the larger part of the hips and not extend beyond them. If the abdomen protrudes, measure from side seam to side seam, across the front. Add the needed amount, plus ½″ or ¾″ for easing across the abdomen. Regardless of whether the abdomen protrudes or not, always ease about ½″, or more if necessary, across skirt front at the waistline.

If the back of the skirt needs enlarging, use the same method. A three-gore skirt pattern is easier to alter for the beginner. Divide the needed amount between the gored seams and side seams. Do not get the center panel too wide. It should equal about one-third the skirt back, from side seam to side seam.

Use the same method when reducing sizes. Do not remove from just one section, but divide amount among seams involved.

Lengthening Pattern Sections

To avoid difficulty in outlining your pattern and dropping darts when lengthening the waist, chalk around the upper portion of the pattern, then move it down 2″, or the amount needed. After dropping the pattern, outline the darts. This will eliminate cutting and pasting of the pattern. Use this method for lengthening sleeves and bust darts. Keep in mind that *measurements must always be accurate.*

Dropped Right or Left Shoulder

Check right and left shoulder from waist to neck. Often the right shoulder is one or two inches lower than the left. This causes the right hip to be one or two inches higher than the left. To correct this, sew the shoulder seam deeper and cut the armscye deeper under the arm to give plenty of freedom for the sleeve. Cut the waist a little shorter on the same side and taper to nothing at the center back. Place a little more padding at the shoulder, so that shoulders appear more even.

Curve the side seam in a little more at the waist, to 4″ or 5″ below the waist. Stitch the right side deeper and straighter, from 2″ to 3″ below waist to hem.

Always baste a straight line thread of a contrasting color on the grainline at the center front of the skirt for a guide mark. See dotted lines on Fig. 192. When the skirt is fitted, the center basting thread will tell if it is hanging straight. If it curves to one side or the other, the skirt is uneven. Raise the waist on one side, and then the other until the center basting thread hangs perfectly straight. A perfectly fitted skirt, or garment, is comfortable and a pleasure to wear.

Sleeve Problems

Differences in arm length: Measure each arm separately from shoulder cap to wrist, with elbow bent; rarely do the arms measure the same length. Check the elbow darts on each sleeve.

When lengthening sleeves, be sure

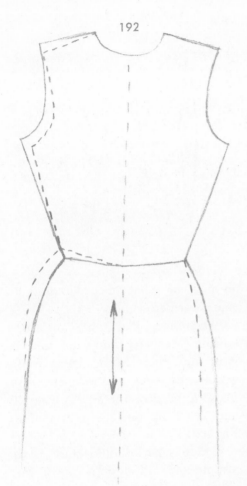

192

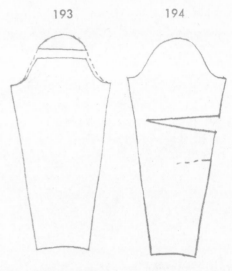

193   194

moved from the length, it can be folded up at the hem, then trim away a small portion at the wrist, tapering toward the elbow.

Prominent Ball and Socket

Slash across cap at point where increase is needed. Separate pattern and gradually extend edge from cap to underarm seam, Fig. 193.

Large Underarm

Slash between elbow dart and underarm edge of sleeve. Spread before cutting.

Ease increased amount in this area, Fig. 194.

Large Elbow

Slash through dart to center, toward top of sleeve and spread the necessary amount. Divide increased

the elbow is in the center of the alloted fullness, or in line with the dart; then increase the length of sleeve where it is needed. Cut in half and pin, or glue, pieces of paper to sleeve sections.

When shortening a sleeve, place alterations according to elbow position and place the fold above or below the elbow, or both, if necessary. If the sleeve only needs an inch re-

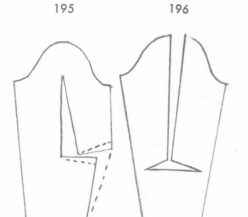
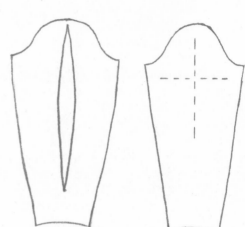

width between two darts, instead of one, Fig. 195.

Large Upperarm

Slash from cap to elbow, toward each side of sleeve and spread the necessary amount.

In doing this the bodice pattern will have to be enlarged under the arm the same amount as was added to the sleeve, half to the front and half to the back section, Fig. 196.

Large Upperarm Muscle

Slash from center of pattern on grain-line, from ⅛″ of center of sleeve cap to approximately 2 or 3 inches from wrist. Spread amount needed and fold darts in cap until pattern lies flat, Fig. 197.

This material does not cover all fitting problems, but it will give you an idea of what must be done to achieve a perfect fit.

Remember: Place a contrasting basting thread on the center front of grain-line, then try to balance the garment perfectly on the figure. Also, place a basting thread horizontally and vertically on sleeve grain-lines, Fig. 198.

• Side seams should start at the armpit and fall directly down each side.

• Shoulder seams should be in line with the neck, approximately ½″ behind the ear.

• The sleeve seam should not extend beyond the shoulder cap.

Study the figure carefully and adjust the pattern accordingly.

Darts should stop below and above the bust, and point toward the bust when they are under the arm and at the waist. Their only function is to fit the curves and contours of the body.

QUESTIONS

1. Name three important factors in creating a well-tailored garment.
2. Why are foundations necessary in a garment?
3. What type of material is used for foundations?
4. Explain the methods of fitting a pattern.
5. Why are darts used? Where are they placed?
6. What is the first step in fitting a skirt?
7. What do you do if a skirt hangs to one side?
8. How are patterns lengthened without cutting?
9. How do you alter a pattern for a low shoulder? Does this affect the fitting of the skirt?
10. What should you check carefully on long sleeves?
11. How can you alter the pattern for a prominent ball and socket?
12. How do you alter the pattern for a large elbow?
13. When altering for a large upper arm, what steps are required?
14. How do you alter the pattern for a large upper arm muscle? How does this affect side seams and darts?

Assembling Pattern and Cutting Garment

Never cut a garment on a small table. If a large cutting table is not available, buy a large piece of pressed board, or heavier board to place on top of a small table. To conserve storage space, cut the board in half and use hinges. If this is not possible, use the floor for a cutting area. This is hard on the knees and back, but a wonderful exercise for stretching the waistline!

Finding the Nap

Drape the material in front of body to decide which way the nap is to run. Satins, velvets and corduroys have a darker sheen when the nap runs up; they "scar" more easily than when the nap runs toward the hemline. The nap may run up or down, depending on individual taste. *Note:* Cut all pieces in the *same direction.*

Rub the back of your hand up and down the fabric. (The palm is too calloused to feel how the nap of the materials lays if the pile of the fabric is very light.) When rubbing against the nap, the material will look scarred, or darker in color.

Place the fabric so the nap runs toward the floor, or hemline, for smoothness and wearability. To obtain a darker sheen in velvets, corduroy, satin, or any nap fabric, cut the material so the nap runs *up* the garment, or toward the shoulders. Heavy napped fabrics such as fleece, hair, woolen faced cloth, and imitation furs, should always run *toward* the hemline.

Cutting the Material

If you are cutting material on the floor where thumbtacks cannot be used, pin the selvedges and ends of material to paper to obtain the true

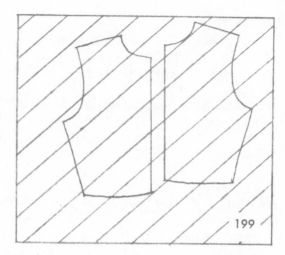

"*In cutting fabric with a diagonal weave, the diagonal line
should run from the . . .*"

square of the woof and warp grain at each end. The kitchen linoleum is best for this job. The material may also be pinned to a woolen rug or carpet.

The pattern will have arrows marking the direction in which it is to be laid. There are three basic directions to work with in cutting out a garment:

• Warp grain that runs parallel with the selvedge.

• *Woof,* or *weft,* grain that runs across the material.

• *Bias* grain, obtained by bringing the cross-grain to meet the selvedge.

• *Diagonal* fold, which will be the *true* bias.

When possible, cut the garment with the material folded. Should the style of the pattern require cutting with material open, be sure to cut pattern sections so they are in pairs, especially if it is a napped fabric.

In cutting fabric with a diagonal weave, the diagonal line should run from the right knee to the left shoulder unless the pattern calls for an unusual design. Pieces should be one continuous line from right to left side of the garment, Fig. 199.

It is of the utmost importance to *cut a garment on the straight grain of the material,* or it will never fit properly or hang straight. When cutting silk or any sheer material, first pin the material to a paper after it has been smoothed and squared in several places.

The detailed instruction sheets included with commercial patterns will help in laying out the pattern. It is advisable for a beginner to follow these instructions, or follow the instructions in this tailoring manual.

Buy one-third or one-half yard of extra material when sewing nap fabrics—even if the pattern does not call for this extra yardage. The nap always requires that the pattern be

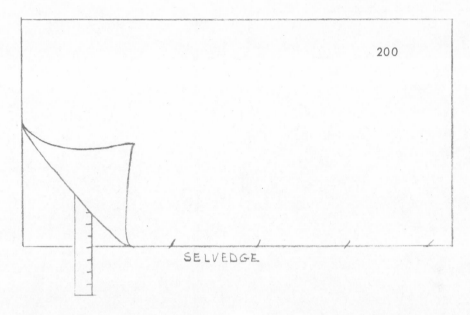

SELVEDGE

200

laid in one direction and a little extra material will often be advantageous.

Lay material flat on the cutting table, full length, before cutting out the garment. Smooth out all wrinkles, with right sides facing inside fold. Keep selvedge edges facing the body, and smooth fabric toward folded edge, away from the body. Trim the end even with the cross-grain by pulling weft thread, if fabric cannot be torn. Fasten to table with thumbtacks. Whip the other ends of the material gently to loosen the two folds if working with wool, because wool is a living fiber and has a tendency to cling. Run a yardstick between the folded fabric to release the wool fibers, Fig. 200. Smooth out and clip the selvedge edges about 12″ apart; pin the two selvedges together, placing pins at right angles to the edge.

Decide which style of garment to use, and count pattern pieces to make sure all are there. When in doubt about the fabric nap, lay pattern pieces on the material all in one direction to check the amount of material before cutting any section. Be sure the right sides of material face inside. If material is warped it will have to be dampened and tacked down for straightening. Sometimes this can be done by steam pressing.

After pattern pieces have been spaced properly, weight them down with sandbag weights, Fig. 201; weights can be made from unbleached muslin in various shapes and sizes. Kitchen cutlery may also serve this purpose. (See Sandbag Weights, page 16, and drawing page 88.)

With tape measure, or yardstick, measure from grain-line of pattern to

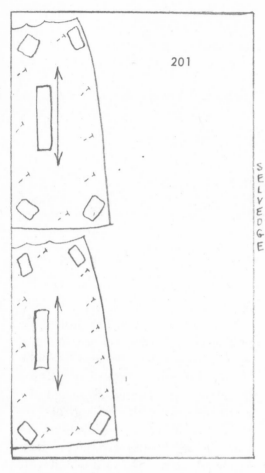

201

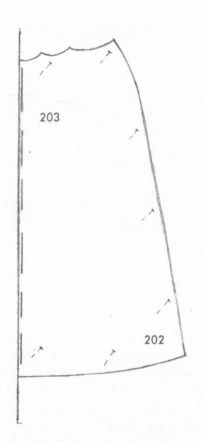

203

202

SELVEDGE.

selvedge edge to be sure pattern is straight, or grain arrow matches grain-line of fabric. This is very important in constructing a properly balanced garment.

Garments that are carefully marked, tailor tacked, and cut are speedily constructed, and time is saved.

Chalk around each pattern piece with tailor's clay chalk, and mark darts and guide marks. To do this, perforate pattern at guide marks, and

work with chalk through perforation. At notches in pattern, place chalk mark on fabric, extending beyond cutting edge of section. Avoid using colored chalk, as the dye is often hard to remove.

After all pattern sections are marked, remove one at a time and tailor tack before cutting into garment pieces. Tailor tacking helps hold the two pieces of cloth together.

Put odd guide marks in different colors of yarn. This makes it easier to match sections.

If chalking around the pattern sections is not desired, pin them all in one direction to prevent ripples in the material. Fig. 202. Put a row of basting on the straight grain in center of pattern section for balancing when trying on garment, Fig. 203.

Baste a little cross of threads about 6″ down on the weft and warp thread in the center of upper sleeve. Leave this in and use it in fitting the sleeve into the garment. When sleeve is perfectly balanced this mark will form a cross. (See Lengthening Pattern Sections, Fig. 198, page 84.)

When cutting out pattern, use long slashing strokes with the scissors. Short snips will cause a crooked, choppy seam. The long strokes are especially recommended when cutting sheer materials which have been attached to paper. Cut through both paper and material. When cutting heavy coat material it is better to cut in a single piece rather than on the fold. Lay pattern pieces out as usual, weight and mark, tailor tack, then cut top layer first. Repeat by cutting underneath layer.

After cutting out each section, group the jacket and skirt sections together. Lay aside collar, cuffs, facings, pockets, etc. This speeds the process of basting for a fitting. Label each section of garment with chalk on wrong side to keep the section identified. This is especially necessary when the right and wrong sides of material are identical.

When cutting garments with lapels, cut the front about ½″ larger from collar notch to bottom of the jacket. This is important because the edges become frayed when pad-stitching the lapels, Fig. 204. Later the fronts are placed together and shaped by trimming this amount away. (See Construction, Garment Interfacings, page 92.)

Cut top collar ⅛″ larger all around the pattern, or pin on material and cut before joining to garment. This insures ease for top collar, and is not trimmed away.

The under collar is always cut on

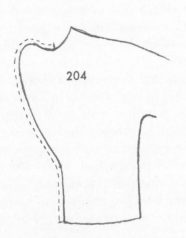

204

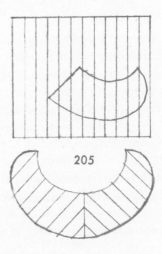

205

the bias with the seam in the center of back, so that opposite sides of the collar roll and lie in the same position. Always cut attached under collar in this manner, regardless of pattern instructions, Fig. 205, page 89.

Cutting Fabric with All-over Design

Always place pattern so the design will be centered in each section, if possible, especially if the design is large. Sometimes it is more effective to place the material so the design is on the left shoulder, right hip, and left hemline. Large floral designs are more attractive if placed on the left shoulder, lower right bodice, left front hip, and lower right knee of skirt. Study the back sections and plan placement of design in the same manner. Study the material carefully before cutting. Take time to drape the material on the body, to select the best placement of design to complement the figure.

Matching Stripes

Use care in choosing a pattern for striped material. Four-gored skirts are best suited for this material, or sheath dresses with very few seams. Place the pattern so that the stripes match in all directions, unless you have an uneven stripe. Do not fold the material. Carefully match the notches on the stripes in each section. Study carefully before each cutting so the stripes will build a pyramid when stitched together. If work-

ing with uneven stripes, check the design carefully and cut each section separately to be sure the design forms a pleasing effect. This requires more yardage than evenly striped fabric. Uneven stripes are more pleasing to the eye when darker, or heavier, stripes are placed toward the hemline.

In cutting suit pieces, plan to have a continuous pattern from jacket to skirt hem, unless using bias binding of self-fabric for trim.

Matching Plaids

A beginner should not try to make a plaid garment. This often tries the patience of an expert. If the plaid consists of uneven stripes, place the larger or darker stripe toward the hemline, unless the style states otherwise. Choosing a pattern with the least amount of seams is wisest. Place all pattern pieces in one direction, then square them with the straight grain markings. Make sure the front and back markings are on the same plaid. The plaid pattern at the crown of the sleeve should match the plaid which runs across the front sections of garment—at the point where notches meet.

There are several methods for matching plaids. One is to baste the sections together with small stitches. Back stitch where the prominent plaids meet so they will not slip while being machine stitched. *Note:* Always machine stitch in the *opposite direction* from which sections were basted.

Another method is to press one

206

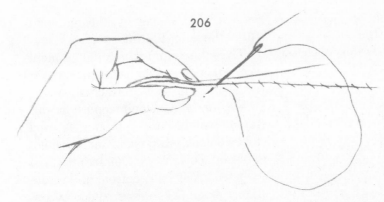

". . . slip baste from right side, creasing seam between thumb and . . ."

seam on stitching line. Lay pressed seam on stitching line of unpressed seam, slip baste from right side, creasing seam between thumb and forefinger, and matching plaid carefully while basting, Fig. 206.

If the machine will sew over pins or small needles, place pins in seams to match plaids, or checks, on pressed half of seam. Fig. 207. After they are matched, reach underneath material and place pins through seam margins so seams will lie flat for machine stitching, Fig. 208. After stitching, turn to right side and remove the pins. Press both seams open and check plaids to be sure they are matched.

There are other methods for matching plaids, but these three are the most practical and reliable.

QUESTIONS

1. Where is it recommended that you cut garments?
2. How can you find the nap of fabric?
3. Which way does the nap run on fleece?
4. What do you do when you can't find the nap?
5. How do you prepare material for cutting?
6. What does warp grain mean?
7. How do you cut a diagonal weave?
8. What is the most important factor in cutting a garment?
9. How do you place material on the table for cutting?

207

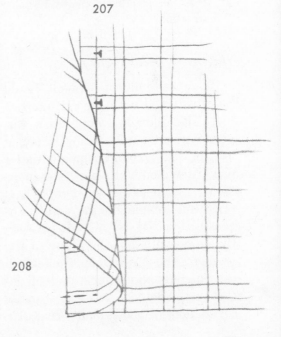

208

10. What do you do if material is warped?
11. Give two methods for anchoring pattern to the material.
12. When do you tailor tack sections of a garment?
13. What kind of scissors do you use? How are they used?
14. How do you cut heavy coat materials?
15. Why is the center front cut ½ inch larger in suits and coats?
16. Where should large designs appear on a garment?
17. What style of garment is best suited for stripes?
18. What is an important factor to consider when cutting suits of striped fabric?
19. What style of garment is best suited for plaids?
20. What must be considered in matching sleeves in plaid garments?
21. How do you baste plaids for construction?

Garment Interfacing

Every well-tailored garment should be constructed with a good interfacing. The difference between a garment without an interfacing, or one of inferior quality, will be apparent after only a few hours of wear. The interfacing is called the *foundation,* and upon this foundation the garment is constructed. It is placed between the outer cloth and the lining of the garment, and has a definite effect on the comfort, appearance, and life of the garment. A well-constructed foundation, of good quality material, retains the shape of the garment throughout its lifetime.

The fabric from which the garment is made determines the type of material used in the interfacing.

• *Haircloth,* which comes in different weights and qualities, is used for woolens, worsteds, and blended wools. This is a combination of worsted, goat hair, cotton, and sometimes linen. The best quality contains a high percentage of worsted and goat hair. Percentages are given on the label. Quality haircloth, crushed in the hand, will immediately spring back to its original shape. Poorer grades retain wrinkles and must be pressed back into shape.

• *Nurses cloth interfacing,* a permanently firm and washable fabric, is best for cotton cord and other cottons.

• *Permanent finish organdy* is an excellent interfacing for ladies' lightweight suits and dresses, and small children's coats.

• *Wigan,* a plain weave cotton cloth, is principally used for pocket, sleeve, and buttonhole interfacings.

• *Silesia cotton twill* is the best pocket material. It is a strong, close-woven twill with a glossy finish on the face, and comes in different weights.

• *Collar interfacing* is a specially prepared linen that can be permanently shaped.

• *Tape,* for staying fronts, is made of linen, cotton, or silk.

There are many synthetic interfacing fabrics on the market, but these should be thoroughly tested before use, since some do not retain a permanent, crisp finish.

QUESTIONS

1. Why are interfacings necessary?
2. What type of interfacing would be desirable for wool, cotton, and silk?
3. Describe the various collar interfacings.
4. What is the function of stay tape?

Skirts

Skirt styles from which to choose are many and varied. The *four-gore skirt* is probably the most popular. The number of gores may be increased as much as desired in order to construct a more flared skirt. Gored skirts may be flared from the waist, or the gores may be fitted over the hip and flared to the hemline.

The *gathered skirt* is quite simple in construction. No fitting is necessary, and all seams are straight. The fullness of the skirt is determined by the amount of material shirred, or gathered, on the waistband. Use nylon thread in the bobbin for shirring; it is stronger and not likely to break. Sew two rows for shirring along the top edge of the skirt. The first should be on the seam allowance line, the second nearer the skirt edge.

The *circular skirt* is another type of full skirt. If the fabric is wide enough, the skirt may be cut in one piece. However, most fabrics are not this wide, in which case the skirt should be cut as two semi-circles. This forms a 2-piece circular skirt with a seam at each side, or one seam in front and one in back. A circular center piece is removed to form the waist of the skirt. To determine the amount of material needed, add one-third of the waist measurement to twice the length of the skirt desired, plus the amount of hem allowance. Place selvedge edges together and find the center, Fig. 209. Mark off one-third of waist measurement at center, Fig. 210. Measuring from center line, mark a semi-circle one-half this center waist measure, Fig. 211. Mark skirt length, plus hem allowance, from waist to lower edge at various points, Fig. 212. In cutting out the circle for the waist, be sure to leave ½″ seam allowance, Fig. 213. This forms a complete circle skirt. In making a two-piece circular skirt, be sure to add side, or center, and back seam allowance.

A variation of this skirt can be made by cutting the waist in a rectangular shape instead of circular. In this case, the center waist measurement remains the same, Fig. 214, but the waist measurement from the center point down is one-third of this amount, Fig. 215. Add seam allowance and clip to corners, Fig. 216. Pleat as shown in Fig. 217. Figs. 209 through 216 appear on the following page. All circular skirts should be allowed to hang at least 48 hours before hemming.

There are many types of *pleated skirts*. The vent-type pleat at front

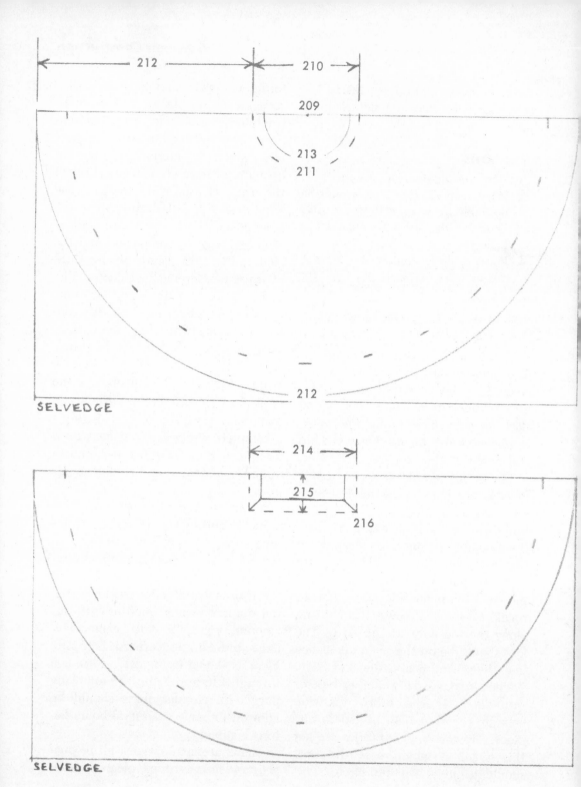

SELVEDGE

SELVEDGE

94

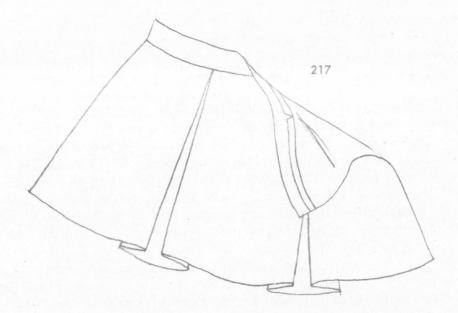

217

and back seam gives slim lines and walking ease. Instead of a vent pleat, an inverted box pleat may be used. Many inverted box pleats may be made around the waist of the skirt. The size of the pleat may vary according to waist measurements, or individual taste. Knife pleated skirts have uniform sized pleats, all running in the same direction. There are variations of this style, such as three stacked knife pleats backed up against three knife pleats running in the opposite direction, which gives a box-pleat effect.

A *straight skirt* is devoid of pleats, but is darted to follow the contour of the hips. It has a tendency to "crawl" when worn in a sitting position. Unless vents or side openings are introduced to the design, this type of skirt does not provide walking ease.

How to Make Full Linings for Skirts (Front and Back)

Completely lined garments are always preferable to unlined garments for the following reasons:
• A lining makes a garment more comfortable, and better fitting.
• Eliminates the need for an underslip.
• Strengthens the garment and helps retain its shape.
• Eliminates crease wrinkles across the front and back.
• Makes the garment shadow-proof, and keeps it from clinging to the body.

Cut the lining just like the skirt pattern, to the crease of hem. Use taffeta lining material of lingerie weight, which will not cling to wool. Other fabrics that may be used for this purpose are cotton sheath, cotton batiste, wigan, silesia, broadcloth, and drapery sateen. When lining washable garments, be sure lining fabric can be washed the same as the garment fabric.

Lay lining front over skirt front; baste down center and around all sides, approximately 2″ from the edge. Baste skirt and fit to body, making any fitting alterations necessary. Baste down center of darts, ½″ beyond finishing point through both skirt and lining. Crease darts on center basting and baste for machine stitching. To stitch darts by machine, lower needle of machine into feeder and butt fabric against needle at point of dart. Stitch toward waist, just barely catching fabric and gradually easing into width of dart, Fig. 218.

When skirt back has gores, or center back seam, complete skirt back before attaching back lining. Join skirt front and skirt back on zipper side seam to zipper opening. Press seams open and insert zipper. Check back lining with skirt back to be sure gores and back sections are of uniform size.

After darts and seams of back lining have been completed, place back lining over front lining, right sides

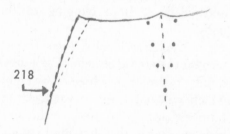

218

facing. Stitch side seams by machine, being careful not to catch top skirt in this operation. Press skirt and lining seams open. Lay back lining over skirt to check fitting of seams and darts. Lay back lining over front lining. Permanently stay-baste lining and skirt side seams, raw seams facing, using one inch stitches of double white basting thread. Start with a knot and end with a knot, keeping basting stitches close to machine stitching of seams, Fig. 219. Bring lining back dart and skirt back dart together and permanently stay-baste. Bring center seam of back lining to meet center seam of skirt back, and permanently baste in the same manner, starting and ending with a knot. Permanently baste dart at other side of skirt back. Before closing last seam of skirt, baste lining to the tape of slide fastener. This can be hand-finished later. Be careful not to pull lining too tightly; it might cause a pucker, or "bubble," on the right side of skirt.

Both box and vent pleats are handled in the same manner. Lining and skirt seams are permanently basted together to pleat opening as on side seam. Clip in to seam of lining and turn pleat extension to the right side, Fig. 220. Fold pleat back and trim pleat extension away to form continuous seam allowance. Baste, press, and catch-stitch crease of lining seam allowance to crease of skirt pleat, being sure stitches are invisible from the right side, Fig. 221. Fold pleat back

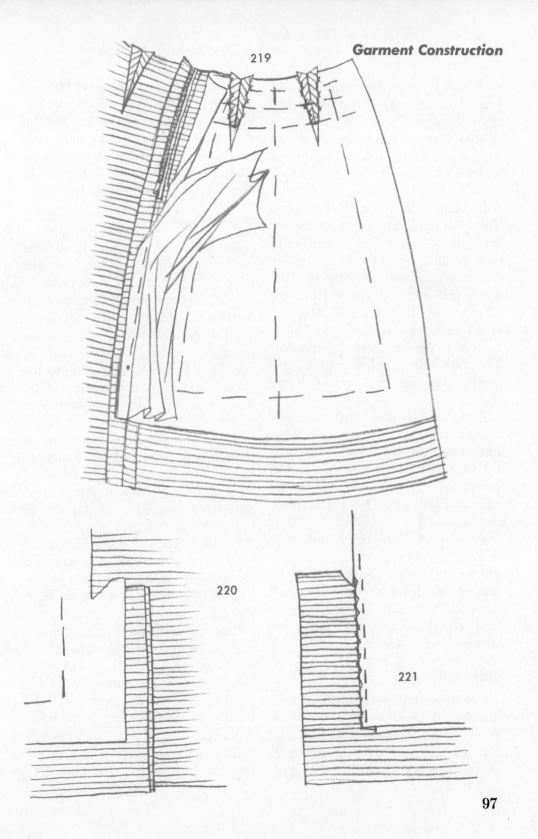

219

220

221

as it will be worn permanently, and baste across the top and down to the end of lining.

Fold lining back and out of the way, and join right seam of skirt front and back together. Press seam open on seam board. Remove basting that holds lining to front skirt section. Take the open left lining seam and bring back to meet the open front seam of lining—right sides facing.

Before machine stitching the last seams of lining and garment be sure all seams will be concealed. Machine stitch and press seams open. Stay-baste as in previous seam instructions. The skirt will be rolled into a "sausage" shape for closing last lining seam.

Baste lining and skirt together around waist, and machine stitch before attaching band. Be sure this stitching is concealed when band is completed. The lining must be the same size as outer garment when completed.

Press skirt thoroughly; allow it to hang at least 24 hours before completing the hem. This will take the normal stretch out of each fabric, and is especially recommended for the inexperienced seamstress when constructing lined skirts.

Half Linings

Cut from back skirt pattern and machine stitch sections if there are gores. Lay on the front section of skirt and machine stitch, or stay-baste, to side seam margin of skirt back. Proceed with side opposite slide fastener opening. Reach between skirt and lining to turn lining over to back of the skirt, and blind stitch to slide fastener tape. Baste to skirt waist, then continue with band. The lining should extend below fullest part of the hip.

Skirt Bands

To make a 1″ wide band, cut lengthwise strip (including selvedge edge, if possible) 3″ wide and 3″ longer than the waist measure. All belts and straps are stronger when cut from *lengthwise* or *selvedge* of material.

Fold in half with *right side* to the *outside* and press with a press cloth. Be sure to cut and fold accurately in center. Take permanent, stiff innerbelting, trim selvedge thread off if there is one, and shrink by dipping in water and pressing dry. Machine stitch inner belt to selvedge half of skirt band, just off of center crease. Fig. 222.

Lay belt flat with raw edge on the bottom. Lift the selvedge half and chalk along the edge of inner belt as a guide for stitching band to skirt, Fig. 223.

Close slide fastener on skirt and place a chalk mark on seam line of waistband on each side of skirt opening. This forms a guide for sewing band to skirt so the front and back band close at the same point when finished.

Ease some fullness across center front of skirt, starting and ending 2″

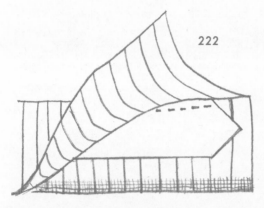

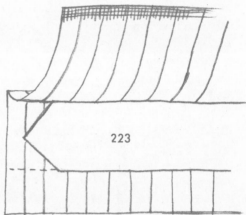

from each side seam. Usually, from ⅝″ to 1″ of ease is necessary to balance a skirt properly, depending on the prominence of the abdomen. Place eased area over ham, dampen seam margin slightly with tip of finger, and press with vertical strokes to shrink before sewing band to skirt. It is best to try on skirt before permanently sewing on band.

Extend 1″ on front end of band at waist and measure 2″ for underlap. Pin, or baste, outside of band to right side of skirt, *using raw edge*, not selvedge of band. Stitch on marked seam allowance, as shown in Fig. 223, when stitching band to skirt.

Have skirt facing feeder of machine and band on top. This method will automatically ease skirt onto band.

Fold band in half, slipping inner belt under skirt and band seam margin. Be sure seam margins face the body. Baste back of band laying flat with selvedge exposed, or hanging free into skirt.

Clip band seam at slide fastener so

the seams can be turned under at the back underlap, and shape the front into a point.

Cut inner belt to form a point on the front, and baste in place. If top stitching is preferred, stitch from the right side on the edge of belt next to the skirt. When no visible stitching is preferred, stitch skirt just off of band into skirt. This will catch the underside of the band but the stitching will not show from the right side.

When no top stitching is used, leave a long thread from your machine stitching at band where point will be finished. Thread needle with this thread and finish point by hand or, when using top stitching, sew around point with machine, Fig. 224. Leave end of underlap unfinished, and merely overcast to eliminate bulk.

Closing Skirt Band

A worked buttonhole may be used in front, and a button on the back of the skirt band if desired.

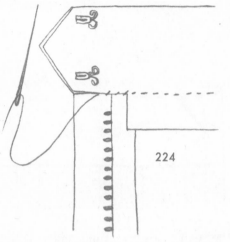

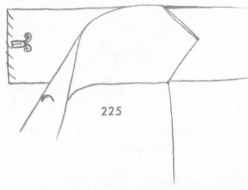

224

225

For a smoother and neater appearance, hand-worked loops and hooks are best. Sew a hook on each side of the point of skirt band, then close slide fastener and lay front band over back to mark for hand-worked loops, and finish. (See How to Make Thread Loops, page 42). Fasten skirt band and sew hook on end of underlap, measuring on front band for loop, Fig. 225.

Skirts with Extended Waist

On skirts with an extended waist instead of attached band, a firm interfacing should be cut, using skirt pattern, extending 4″ or 5″ below normal waistline, minus seam allowances. Machine stitch darts in skirt, slash, and press open. On interfacing, cut out these same darts on stitching line. Lay interfacing over wrong side of skirt, butting cut edges of interfacing darts against sewn edges of skirt darts.

Catch-stitch pressed open dart to interfacing; press side seams back over interfacing, and catch-stitch. Finish skirt top in same manner, leaving bottom section unattached. By attaching interfacing by hand, bulky seams are eliminated.

To insure a smooth fit of this type of waist, fit skirt to find natural waistline. Slash interfacing across skirt front only at waistline, and catch-stitch slashed pieces together. This will keep interfacing from buckling with action of the body, Fig. 226.

This type of interfacing is also very effective when used in fitted sheath dresses.

In a skirt in which the waistband is eliminated, grosgrain ribbon makes a good skirt stay. Catch-stitch ribbon flat on seam margin at waist, turn down into skirt, and catch-stitch to interfacing as previously discussed. Without an interfacing or skirt lining, there is nothing to which to attach this stay except the seams at waistline. Finish with skirt lining either underneath or on top of grosgrain band.

100

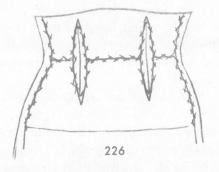

226

When using this type of stay inside a sheath dress, leave open at slide fastener end and close with a hook and eye.

QUESTIONS

1. Name three styles of skirts and give a brief summary of construction.
2. How can you change the syle of a circular skirt?
3. What is a vent pleat, a box pleat, and a knife pleat?
4. Why are fully lined skirts preferred to unlined?
5. What type of fabric is recommended for linings?
6. How do you cut a skirt lining?
7. What section of lining is attached to the skirt first? How?
8. When do you insert the slide fastener?
9. Give a brief summary of skirt construction after the slide fastener is in.
10. Explain cutting and attaching of a skirt half-lining.
11. How wide is an average skirt band unfinished, finished?
12. Describe the steps involved in preparing a skirt band.
13. Which end of skirt band is longer?
14. How do you conceal top stitching on a skirt band?
15. What type of closure is preferable on bands?
16. How are skirts with extended waistbands finished?
17. What is the procedure when a waistband is eliminated?
18. What is meant by a dress stay?

Pleats

Tailoring calls for many pleats in skirts, dresses, jackets, and some styles of coats. Some pleats look so bulky the garment would have a better appearance without them, but they serve a necessary purpose in allowing freedom of movement, and are a functional part of the garment.

Accuracy in the sewing of pleats is essential or the garment will not hang straight, or fit well.

Select pleat styles that flatter the figure. Pleats stitched and pressed toward the center of the body have a slenderizing effect, while those pressed away from center add width.

Finishing Hems with Pleats

Stitch seams to crease of hem. Turn up with raw edges exposed, and stitch hem in seam to hold it in place.

Overcast, buttonhole stitch, or zigzag raw edges of hem and seams together. Hems completed in this manner hang evenly, eliminating that bulky look, and stay neatly pressed.

Kick Pleat or Fly Pleat

This type of pleat is part of the fold

101

in the skirt or skirt seam. The fold is usually pressed to the left side of the skirt, and stitched as if doing a tuck, Fig. 227. If the front or back is in one piece, finish the hem and press thoroughly. Stitch on crease of pleat from wrong side after final pressing, Fig. 228. Turn to right side and stitch pleat closure through right side, or leave open to give a tucked effect.

If there is a seam in the pleat, close the seam by machine to the point where the hem is finished, or to the crease of the hem. Baste and press pleat in place and stitch by machine. Finish hem, starting at pleat and ending at pleat, with hem seams open and the raw edge exposed. When finished and pressed, baste or pin hem with edges together and machine stitching exposed. Clip corner of seam allowance at crease of hem, Fig. 229. Over-

cast raw seam of hem by hand, serge, or zigzag stitch by machine. Hems finished in this manner lay smooth and never appear bulky from the right side.

When seams are trimmed and the pleat extended on the wrong side, in unlined garments, reinforce the pleat. Cut a piece of silk about 8 inches long, on the straight of the material, as wide as the pleat. Stitch to top of the pleat by machine and slip under seam margin. Catch-stitch silk to seam margin to keep stitches invisible on the right side of garment, Fig. 230.

This reinforcement may be attached to the waist or just a few inches above the pleat. Loosely catch-stitch to the garment, or machine stitch with the waist seam. A reinforcement carried to the waistline is generally most satisfactory.

227

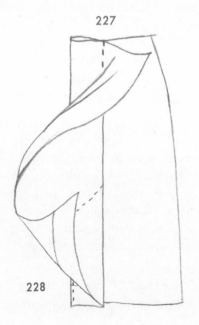

228

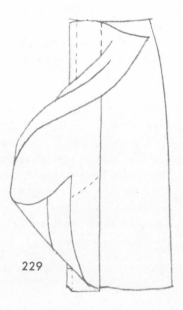

229

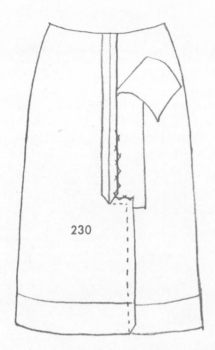

230

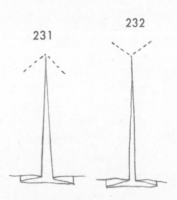

231   232

Apply this crease stitching to all pleats, tucks, and darts. The results will be amazing!

If desired, machine stitch arrow at pleat opening for trim and reinforcement, Figs. 231 and 232.

Box Pleats or Inverted Pleats

This pleat is usually part of the front or back skirt panel, or it could be two kick pleats facing each other with a seam in the center.

Baste on stitching line of pleat all the way to the hemline. Machine stitch to pleat opening and tack thread.

Press tuck flat to form a box pleat. Baste firmly, before stitching pleat from right side. Stitch in center of pleat so stitching will be concealed, or stitch ¼″ on each side of the center for welt trim. Allow bastings to remain in skirt until completed, pressed, and ready to wear. Crease-stitch by machine on the wrong side of pleats. This keeps the pleats in place with fewer pressings.

Inverted Pleat with Underlay

This pleat is decorative as well as useful. It adds width to narrow skirts, and requires less yardage than inverted pleats cut without seams. However, it is more bulky than pleats cut on the fold of fabric.

Join garment sections together to opening of pleat, then baste fold line by hand and press seams open. Place underlay on top of pleat extension, right sides of the material facing, and baste firmly in place, Fig. 233. If top stitching is not desired, start stitching skirt and underlay at seam stitching, doing each side separately, Fig. 234. Catch-stitch top of pleat to skirt, being careful to keep stitches invisible on right side. When skirt is lined, catch-stitch into lining only.

103

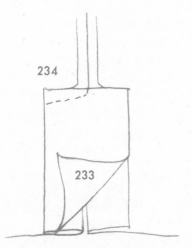

234

233

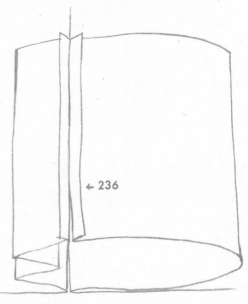

← 236

235

If pleat is stitched down on the right side of skirt, join sides of skirt and underlay. Press and catch-stitch together until finished, then turn on right side and baste firmly before stitching across top of the underlay. To strengthen pleat at opening, see reinforcement instructions in Kick or Fly Pleats, pages 101 and 102.

Double Inverted Pleat with Slit at Hem

This pleat requires a seam at the center. The number of pleats used, should be determined by the weight of the fabric.

Measure carefully for size and number of pleats before cutting, Fig. 235. Remove bastings and trim away fold of pleats about 4 inches above slash opening, being sure to leave a seam allowance. Close seam permanently to slash opening, Fig. 236. Baste pleats in place and machine stitch across top of pleat, *but not through garment*.

When a skirt is unlined, a pleat stay should be used. Place a piece of light-weight fabric (lining), under center back seam, the width that pleats will be finished, reaching from waistline to top of pleats, Fig. 237. Catch-stitch seam margin to pleat stay, or lining, and lay pleats on top of stay after they have been stitched together. Feather stitch pleat to pleat stay across top and about 1″ down the sides. If top stitching is desired, stitch pleat to garment by machine, stitching through pleat stay.

Finish hem slightly above slit, starting at slash and ending at slash. This helps to keep slit from splitting open. Fold first pleat back over hem and blind stitch from top to hem crease. If the material frays badly, overcast the raw edge. It may also be blanket stitched, or turned under and crease stitched.

After pleats are constructed and permanently pressed, crease stitch by machine, on wrong side, from top of pleat to end, through hem, Fig. 238. This will help retain a permanent press in pleats.

Pressing Pleats

Pleats should be even and correctly fitted before pressing. Lightly catch-stitch together with silk thread to keep in correct position for pressing. Creases set by pressing are almost impossible to remove.

Chemical and transparent press cloths are available at notion counters. Transparent cloths are helpful in pressing straight pleats. To avoid

an indentation appearing on the right side when pressing pleats, place a piece of tissue under each pleat. Lay a chemical press cloth on top of pleats and dampen with a sponge. Place a second cloth on top of the dampened chemical cloth and press with a medium hot iron, keeping the iron in motion until thoroughly steamed but not dry. When pressing pleats in bulky fabric, or fabric with a heavy nap, use heavy brown paper instead of tissue. Place a scrap of material against the garment, right sides facing, and dampen with a sponge. Over this place a press cloth and press until almost dry. Brush with a stiff brush to raise the nap. For a sharp finish, pound the pleat crease, using a hardwood pounding block while the fabric is still steaming.

Reinforced Vents or Split Seams

Plackets and vents in tailored garments must be reinforced, especially if worn by very active people. To do this, machine stitch, or catch-stitch, a piece of stay-tape to the underneath side of a vent, close to the crease, Fig. 239. Press vent as it will be when finished and catch-stitch together on right side of garment. Catch-stitch extended piece of stay-tape to seam.

Place a second piece of stay-tape on top of seam margin, above clipped seam of vent, and angle slightly over the vent opening. Catch-stitch stay-tape to end of seam allowance, stopping and then starting again after

237

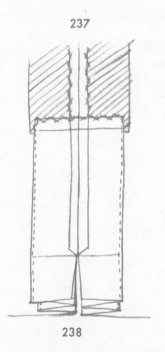

238

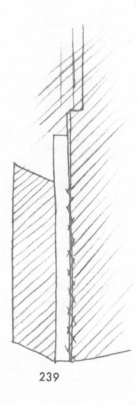

239

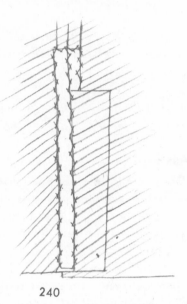

240

for strength, Fig. 241. Ladies' fully-lined skirts with pleat cut away are strengthened when reinforced with stay-tape. Fig. 240.

tape has crossed opening of vent, Fig. 240. Be sure stitches are concealed from the right side. Vents, or pleats, finished in this manner will never stretch out of shape, or tear at the seam junction.

Ladies' narrow skirts also need re-inforcing. Cut a small square of material twice as wide as the seam margin. Fold in half, forming a triangle, machine stitch to the top of vent, or seam, but not through to the right side of the garment. Catch-stitch to seam of garment to keep it in place. Use the same procedure in a skirt slash or split seam. Machine stitch to seam on the wrong side and catch-stitch to seam and top of the triangle

QUESTIONS

1. What is the purpose of pleats? What determines their selection?
2. How should hems with pleats be finished?
3. What is a kick pleat or fly pleat?

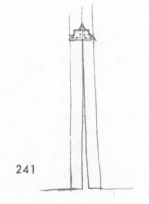

241

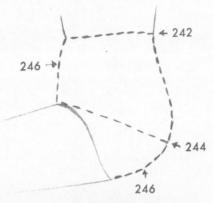

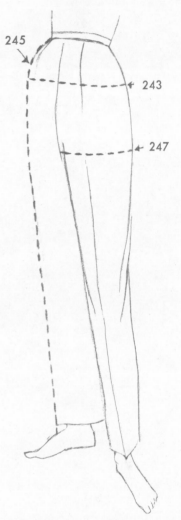

4. Explain the difference between a pleat cut with a seam and one cut on a fold.
5. Explain the box or inverted pleat. How is it finished?
6. How are pleats treated to retain the crease?
7. How is the inverted pleat with underlay prepared?
8. How does the double inverted pleat differ from the inverted pleat?
9. How do you finish the hem of the double inverted pleat?
10. How do you eliminate indentation when pressing?
11. Describe the reinforcement of vents and pleats.
12. What type of pleat reinforcement, other than stay-tape can be used?

Ladies' Slacks

Measure the waist in the same manner as for skirts, Fig. 242. Measure the hips 7″ below the waist, Fig. 243. Then measure hips a second time while seated in a chair, to determine the necessary amount of ease, Fig. 244. Normally, 2″ of ease is required, except in extremely fitted slacks. Tie a belt around the waist and measure outside seam to the floor, when barefoot, Fig. 245. This leaves a small hem. When leaving a side slit opening, increase hem to cover the depth of slit. While seated, measure from crotch to center back of waist for seat depth. Measure the same way in front, and then measure from waist to chair, Fig. 246. Measure upper leg and thigh, Fig. 247. The crotch

107

248

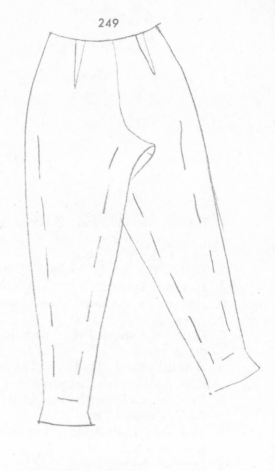

249

depth must be at right angles with crotch seam junctions, Fig. 248. Compare these measurements with pattern pieces before cutting fabric.

Slacks that are completely lined are more comfortable, and more durable, than unlined ones, and they retain their shape permanently.

• Use skirt instructions to join fronts together from waist to crotch.

• Stay-baste to lining.
• Machine stitch front suppression lining and darts together.
• Cut away and catch-stitch lining at the pocket seam.
• Attach pocket, and complete according to pattern instructions.
• Join center back seams and close darts.
• Join side seams, folding lining back out of the way.
• Join inside leg seams. Press open.
• Join center back lining and press seams open.

• Place back lining on top of front lining with right sides facing. Baste from base of pocket to hem on the outside and inside seam, Fig. 249.

• Machine stitch.

• Press open and stay-baste lining and slack seams together.

Follow lined skirt instructions, page 95, for completing slacks. Belt carriers may be stitched on top, or stitched in with band, and the upper end stitched down later.

When placing a slide fastener in center front, put the placket on the right front section.

QUESTIONS

1. How do you measure for crotch depth of ladies' slacks?

2. Give three other important measurements for fitting slacks.
3. Why should slacks be lined?
4. How are linings attached to slacks?

Suit Coats or Jackets

Hold front pattern to the body to determine the natural waistline.

Lay pattern on interfacing fabric on straight of grain, and draw an outline as shown in Fig. 250. Cut curve slash 2″ deep on shoulder, about 2″ from neck. Cut a small slash dart at neck. If bust is large, cut an additional dart into foundation from side toward crest of bust. Cut dart away at natural waistline.

If front pattern is in two pieces, pin

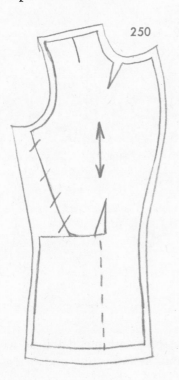

250

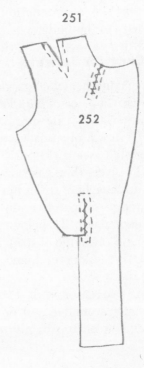

251

252

together at seam line from shoulder
to crest of bust, before constructing
haircloth foundation.

Cut a small, square haircloth patch
to insert under slash at shoulder.
Place patch on wrong side of interfacing.

Match straight of grain on neckside, and spread ½″ toward armscye.
Stitch by machine, close to raw edge,
Fig. 251. Trim patch close to stitching line. See drawing page 109.

When using a slash dart at neck,
butt dart together, and close by
stitching a 1″ strip of wigan, or some
soft fabric, on wrong side of interfacing. Turn to right side and zigzag
raw edges of slash dart to strip of
fabric, Fig. 252, page 109.

Be sure all patches and fabric strips
are on *wrong side* of foundation. They
must be next to the body.

Heavy Coats or Jackets

When making heavy coats, or jackets, cut an extra piece of haircloth and
place on interfacing. Be sure patch is
at least 1″ inside of armscye and 1″
below shoulder seam, Fig. 253. Pin,
or baste in place, then take one strip
of fabric and machine stitch in center,
catching edge of patch and letting
strip extend about 2″ below patch.
Stitch around raw edge of strip. Leave
the other three sides of hymo patch
free, Fig 254.

Pull darts together with 1″ fabric
strips, sewing around edges of strips
and zigzagging on top of raw edges,
Fig. 255.

253

Make felt wadding patch of wool,
or cotton, as indicated, and place on

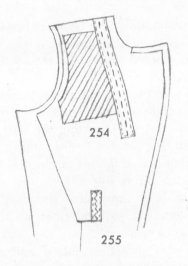

254

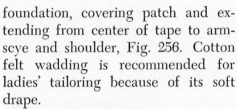

255

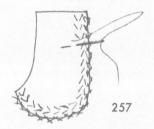

257

scye, Fig. 257. (See Padding Stitch, page 22.) Always work with armscye facing the body. When completely padded, dunk in water and press thoroughly dry on grain-line. Place over tailor's ham, dampen, and press to shape bust.

foundation, covering patch and extending from center of tape to armscye and shoulder, Fig. 256. Cotton felt wadding is recommended for ladies' tailoring because of its soft drape.

Catch-stitch, or zigzag, felt patch to interfacing on inside.

Start pad stitching, or zigzagging, felt patch from center front to arm-

Raglan Interfacings

When cutting foundations for suits, or coats, with raglan sleeves, pin front sleeve to front coat section before cutting. Construct the interfacing as in previous instructions, but cut it as chart indicates, Fig. 258. Do not let foundation extend beyond shoulder cap at any time.

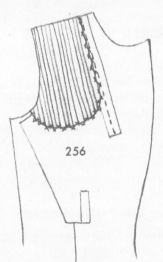

256

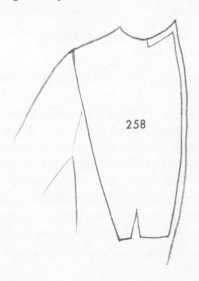

258

111

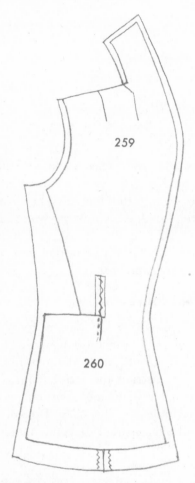

259

260

Roll Collar or Shawl Collar Interfacings

When making interfacings for rolled or shawl collars, extend the interfacing into the collar. When pattern calls for a dart at roll line of collar, slash where the collar extends above the shoulder of garment, about 3″ toward waist, Fig. 259. Overlap and machine stitch flat instead of making ¼″ dart. Complete as shown in previous interfacing instructions.

Shawl collars occasionally have set-

on collars under the facing. (See Collar Instructions, page 131.) The collar is worked separately; then put on by hand.

When placing interfacing around the bottom of a garment, cut the front all in one piece, putting the darts in interfacing at the waist. Slit dart, overlap material, and machine stitch, or catch-stitch, Fig. 260.

Cut back interfacing sections like the garment pattern, from waist to crease of hem.

When garment is fitted and machine stitched, trim interfacing to ease sections under the seams, and catch-stitch seam margin to interfacing. Do not catch-stitch at waistline.

QUESTIONS

1. Explain how interfacing darts are made.
2. Why do patches and strips of fabric face the lining of a garment?
3. How do heavy coat and jacket interfacings differ from those of light-weight garments?
4. What is the final step in the preparation of the interfacing before putting in the garment?
5. Describe the difference between a raglan interfacing and one for a set-in sleeve.
6. Describe the preparation of the interfacing in roll or shawl collars.
7. How is the interfacing attached around the bottom of a garment?

Men's Coat Interfacings

When cutting men's coat interfacings, use garment pattern and cut as shown in Fig. 261. Follow previous instructions to finish interfacing, with the exception that the curved shoulder slash should be spread ⅝".

In men's coats, as in heavy coats, cut an extra piece of haircloth and place on interfacing. (See Fig. 254 in Heavy Coat Section, page 111.)

Cut felt wadding patch to slightly below the waistline if you do not have a pattern, Fig. 262. Catch-stitch on lapel side and across bottom. Pad-stitch, or zigzag, from front toward armscye. Shrink and press as in previous instructions.

Cuff Interfacing

All cuffs are improved by interfacing. Nylon net, nurses linen, taffeta, collar linen, wigan, and permanent organdy are suitable. Cut interfacing from cuff pattern, minus seam margins. If more stiffness is desired, attach two or more layers of interfacing together with parallel machine stitching before attaching to cuff.

Place interfacing on topmost section of cuff. Baste on outer section across the top of cuff, and catch-stitch in place on stitching line. Place running basting line ½" below catch-stitching, Fig. 263, page 114. Fold interfacing back over basting stitch and attach the cuff with drapery basting stitch. The weight of the fabric and size of the cuff should decide the size and spacing of stitches.

After the interfacing is attached, catch-stitch it to the cuff all around

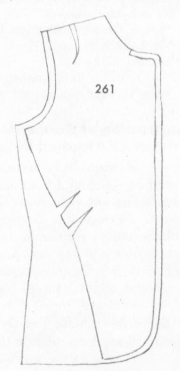

261

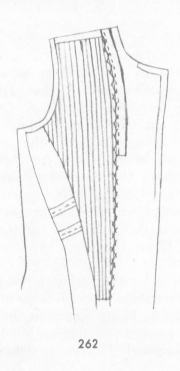

262

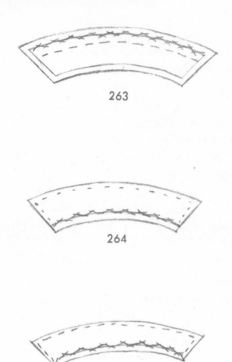

263

264

265

on stitching line. On notched cuff, baste and machine stitch cuff sections together on 3 sides. Trim seams of top section narrower than facing, press open and edge baste. Catch-stitch top cuff seam margins onto facing, keeping stitches invisible. Baste cuff and facing about 1″ from bottom and press. Cut seam margin off cuff facing and catch-stitch to upper cuff. Fig. 264. Miter corners of top cuff and catch-stitch hem to cuff facing, Fig. 265. Press thoroughly and pound seams.

When a cuff is notched, crease ends between thumb and forefinger of left hand with facing uppermost, and attach together with nappery stitch for approximately 1″. Turn to right side.

When the notch is eliminated, interface as instructed previously, close top cuff section and then under cuff section by machine. Attach the two sections together at the upper edge. Complete in the same manner as for a notched cuff.

Finish sleeve hem in usual manner. Baste cuff on sleeve, slightly overlapping creases of sleeve hem, and hand fell to sleeve. This method is advantageous because, when the cuff is removed, the sleeve underneath is completed and the cuff stands up well, without appearing bulky.

QUESTIONS

1. How do interfacings of men's coats differ from ladies'?
2. What type of fabric is recommended for cuff interfacing?
3. How is the interfacing attached?
4. What stitch is used in closing a notched cuff?
5. Why should cuffs be finished before being attached to a sleeve?

Construction of Garments with Notched or Attached Collars

Baste all main body sections together firmly enough for an accurate fitting before any permanent sewing is done. Baste a little deeper than regular seams to keep from machine stitching on top of bastings. Machine stitch as close to bastings as possible for smoother and straighter seams.

Baste the sleeves together but not into the garment; baste from shoulder to hem and machine stitch in the opposite direction. Always sew from hem to waist. This will eliminate sew-ing ease into garment seams which may have been basted into them.

When fitting women's garments, wear shoes of the type which will nor-mally be worn, and a good brassiere and girdle. Otherwise the garment may look and feel as though it were made for another individual.

Use shoulder pads for every fitting. The jacket should be a little snug for the first fitting, because of deeper seams taken when basting. Also, most woolens and worsteds stretch during the final pressing, providing the ma-terial has been needle-shrunk before cutting. Look for wrinkles, fullness, or a bloused look, across the shoulders in the back. These are the most com-mon fitting problems, and if any of them occur, the back will have to be raised.

To raise the back, fold shoulder seams together accurately, and trim across back of neck and down shoul-der seam, tapering toward armscye. If necessary to trim shoulder seam at armscye, it must be trimmed the same amount under the arm. See dotted line, Fig. 266. If one shoulder is lower than the other, trim the front and back shoulder seam as needed, in ex-cess of the amount already removed. If shoulders slope considerably, an equal amount should be trimmed across the top of shoulders.

Check the front to see if the center front guide markings of garment hang perpendicular to the hemline. The front should balance, or stay closed to hemline when you are standing. If

266

the garment spreads apart and ripples and bulges appear, lift at the neckline until it balances vertically on the body. Pin and baste a dart at the neckline to keep the garment in this position, and reshape neck opening. This problem most often occurs with the full-busted figure. If bias wrinkles persist, at side of bust, place dart from crest of bust to side seam. Rebaste for a second fitting before permanently stitching. In fitting a stoop-shouldered person, it is necessary to increase the back shoulder seams to twice the width the pattern recommends, and shorten the front the width of a seam.

Do not extend darts above the crest of the bust. The side darts should point upward toward the crest of the bust. The top button should be slightly above, or below, the crest of the bust. Measure the distance be-tween bust crests and compare with bodice measurements. Alter if neces-sary.

115

Remove garment and separate the front from the back, but leave a few threads in seam for machine stitching guide.

Baste reinforcement strip in back of buttonholes on wrong side of right front. Make buttonholes through this material.

Always reinforce pockets. Finish buttonholes and pockets in front sections while separated unless they get hand-worked buttonholes. Hand-worked buttonholes are more easily and accurately completed when the garment has been completed and pressed.

Buttonholes require a great deal of concentration and, therefore, should not be attempted when tired or under trying circumstances. It is best to practice on a scrap of the fabric with which you are working. Buttonholes are made in the *right front* of ladies' garments, and *left front* on men's garments. Try to make them as neatly as possible because buttonholes, pockets, and collars, are the highlights of a garment.

Complete darts and seams in front sections and press thoroughly on seam board or tailor's ham. (See Placing of Darts, page 81.)

Baste the pocket reinforcement and complete pockets. If a different type of pocket than that indicated on pattern is desired, see section on pockets, page 58.

Basting Foundation to Fronts

Press the shape of the bust in the foundation and fronts of garment over a tailor's ham, before basting. Baste together, with garment top placed on smooth side of foundation. Basting over a tailor's ham may help to retain the shape of the bust.

For ladies' garments, measure and mark lapel break line from shoulder 1″ inside neck edge, to 1″ above top button.

Always have wrong side of the foundation next to the body, and the smooth side toward the exterior of garment.

Baste on break line for lapel padding from shoulder to slightly above first buttonhole, and down the front about 1½″ from the edge. Place left hand under front and foundation at bust point and baste over it to keep this shape permanent. Baste about three rows from top to hemline to keep foundation in place. Angle across the shoulder and baste about 2″ from armscye, following the outline of the foundation. Do not baste ripples in foundation or garment.

If fullness appears in foundation toward side seam, clip into foundation, overlapping clipped edges, and catch-stitch together.

Place a second row of bastings over bust pocket and keep these bastings far enough from raw edges so they will not interfere with joining garment seams for next operation. Press bust with press cloth over a tailor's ham. Check to see if foundation is perfectly smooth.

Try on for second inspection before

basting the bridle strap and pad-stitching lapel at the break line.

A bridle strap is a piece of wigan, or stay-tape, that will not stretch, 1" wide and as long as the roll line; it controls the roll of the revers and holds the garment to the body. For ladies' tailoring, mark 1" inside neck, Fig. 267, to 1" above top button, Fig. 268. Baste bridle strap on lapel roll

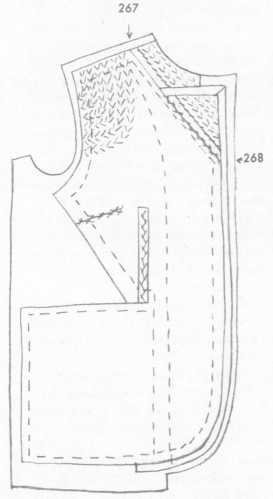

267

268

line by holding strip a little taut. After marking the roll line on garment, mark 1" inside the shoulder seam at the neck to 1" above first, or top, buttonhole on foundation. Always hold garment so the raw edge of the lapel will be facing the body and the lapel lies as it will when worn, before pad-stitching the front lapel and interfacing together. Keep stitches invisible on front of garment, when doing this. Refer to Tailor's Quilting or Padding Stitch, pages 22 and 23.

Start quilting on the right lapel at the shoulder, and on the left, above the buttonhole. The roll of the lapel is made by holding the material firmly, and by keeping the stitches easy. Keep lapels firmly rolled over the hand while pad-stitching. Continue working up and down until lapels are padded, as shown in Figs. 267 and 268. Always keep all four fingers together and use your thumb to control the fabric.

When using sheer wool, or silk suiting material, it is often necessary to line the lapel facing with wigan. This lining should cover only the quilted area of collars and lapels. It prevents the stitches from showing through the facing when the garment is completed and receives the final pressing.

Another method of quilting sheer fabrics is to use drapery basting stitch applied between interfacing and garment. See Drapery Basting, page 29, when using this method to pad a lapel; separate interfacing back to

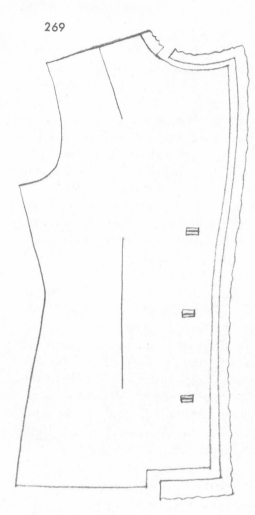

269

for the process of trimming all ragged seams and edges, to give a sharp, clean, look to the garment.

Place the two fronts together with right sides to the outside and buttonhole section on top.

Carefully lay garment on a table or flat surface, and accurately match the two sections before trimming. Use sharp cutting shears.

Check to be sure buttonholes are spaced correctly.

If preferred, the fronts may be pinned together, with pins running in one direction. Trim ¼″ or ½″ starting about 2″ from shoulder seam at the neck to the collar notch. Continue around the lapel, down the front and across the bottom of facing as illustrated, Fig. 269. When making children's garments, leave lining and facing equal lengths, so that the garment can be lengthened as needed. When fronts are trimmed, the distance between stitching line and outside corner of buttonhole should approximately equal the width of buttonhole, plus seam allowance.

Trim the hemline around the jacket or coat separating the fronts, and tailor tack hem crease after side seams are closed.

Apply the same method on shawl collars except that the shoulder will be closed and the side seams open until fronts are finished. This is why an allowance is left on the garment fronts when cutting. Allow ¼″ or ⅜″ seam allowance for suits and never more than ½″ for coats.

basting or roll line, and drapery baste a row from innermost point of roll line. Space rows of drapery basting ¼″ to ½″ apart, always working from left to right. This stitch cannot be done in an up and down manner—a new row must be started each time.

After pad-stitching, dampen the interfacing and lapel, then press.

Shaping the Garment

Shaping is a professional term used

118

After the backs and fronts have been sewn together, tailor tacks may be placed on the hem crease. This line may not be accurate but it will be very helpful in turning up the hem.

Joining Stay-tape to Fronts

After the fronts have been trimmed or made even, reinforce them with stay-tape. Use professional stay-tape, which is especially woven for use in tailoring garments, because it will not stretch and is light in weight. This should not be confused with cotton twill tape. Stay-tape is available in linen, cotton, or linen and cotton combination in ¼″, ⅜″, ½″ widths, etc. One-half inch is preferable because it keeps the seams from becoming too bulky.

Dampen stay tape and press to shrink. The seam allowance should be ¼″ or ⅜″ after shaping. When using tape on curved lapels or hemlines, stretch and press tape into curve while damp. For this reason, it is important to determine the shape of fronts before pressing tape.

The outer edge of tape and hymo cannot be equal. The center of seam tape should straddle the interfacing, leaving about ¼″ or ⅛″ of front seam margin extending beyond the outside edge of the tape, depending upon the width of seam allowance, Fig. 270.

Press the tape before joining to front, Fig. 271. Starting at bridle strap, baste tape from bridle strap past collar notch, continuing around the edge of garment front; hem-crease

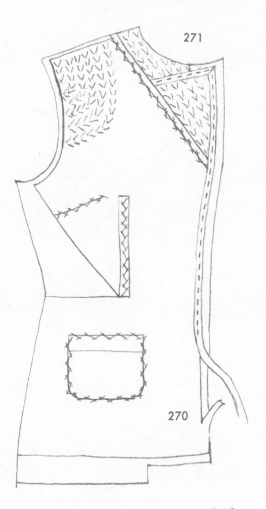

where lining and facing are attached. Bring tape across the bottom of garment the width of the facing.

Miter the corners of tape to insure a smooth seam turn, instead of folding corners. Cut away corners and catch-stitch together.

Press tape again and whip to hymo on the inside edge of tape with medium size stitches, Fig. 272. Do not catch front garment material with tape and interfacing, but whip the

119

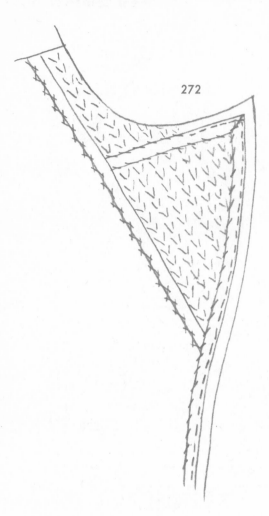

272

tape firmly to interfacing or foundation material. Leave the outside edge of the tape free to machine stitch when joining fronts and facings together.

QUESTIONS

1. Describe the steps in preparing a garment for a trial fitting.
2. What are the most common fitting problems? How can they be corrected?
3. Why is it necessary to check the center front carefully?
4. What determines the placement of darts?
5. Give the order of construction after the fitting is completed.
6. Describe attachment of interfacing to the front, and how to determine the break line of the lapel.
7. How is side fullness of interfacing corrected?
8. What is the function of the bridle strap, and where is it attached?
9. When padding the lapel, how is a garment held? What stitches may be used?
10. Explain the differences in padding of sheer and bulky wools.
11. What step follows the padding of lapels?
12. What is meant by "shaping garment fronts"?
13. Of what importance is the buttonhole in shaping a garment front?
14. How do shawl collars differ from set-on collars?
15. What is the function of stay-tape and how is it attached?
16. When working with tape, is shrinking necessary? How are corners turned?
17. Describe the necessary steps in attaching facings to garment fronts.
18. Why are seams trimmed before edge-basting?
19. How are seams of the front of garment catch-stitched?
20. Why is it necessary to cut windows in the interfacing for buttonholes?
21. How are pockets treated? Why?
22. How is the garment held for diagonal basting?
23. What is necessary for completion of a well-tailored garment?

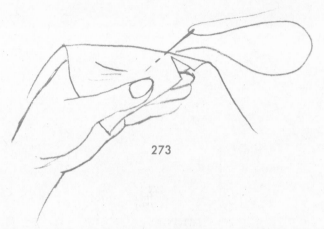

"Place full side over fingers of left hand when basting . . ."

273

24. Where is lapel ease placed, when basting?
25. How do you obtain a hard, sharp finish?

Joining Facings to Fronts

Make sure the lapel is slightly fuller than the front of garment. This insures ease so the lapel will roll properly when garment is completed. Check to see that the facing extends a little beyond the shoulder seam, or even with it. It must not be shorter. Soft woolens require more ease around lapels than worsteds or silks.

With the facing on top, ease ¼″ to ½″ fullness, depending upon the size of lapel, while basting front and facing together. After basting around the lapel, smooth out on a table and baste the remainder as smoothly as possible, or slightly ease the front onto facing below the waist and around the lower corner of facing. Place full side over fingers of left hand when basting, to obtain necessary ease, Fig. 273.

Dampen seam allowance, and using horizontal ironing strokes over a ham, shrink all fullness from lapel. This avoids stitching pleats into seams.

Machine stitch front, facing, and unattached edge of tape all in one operation, staying as close as possible to the edge of the tape. Be sure to stitch fronts and facings evenly.

Clip to machine stitching where the collar joins to lapel before turning, Fig. 274. Press seams open on edge of a seam board, run the iron over seam to spread apart, and then dampen seam with the tip of finger, pressing hard and flat. Press dry.

Graduate the seams by trimming the front seam a generous ⅛″ to ¼″, depending upon the fabric, and the facing ¼″ on the lapel, except around curves, then both seams are trimmed to ⅛″, Fig. 275. Turn to the right side and edge-baste. See page 122.

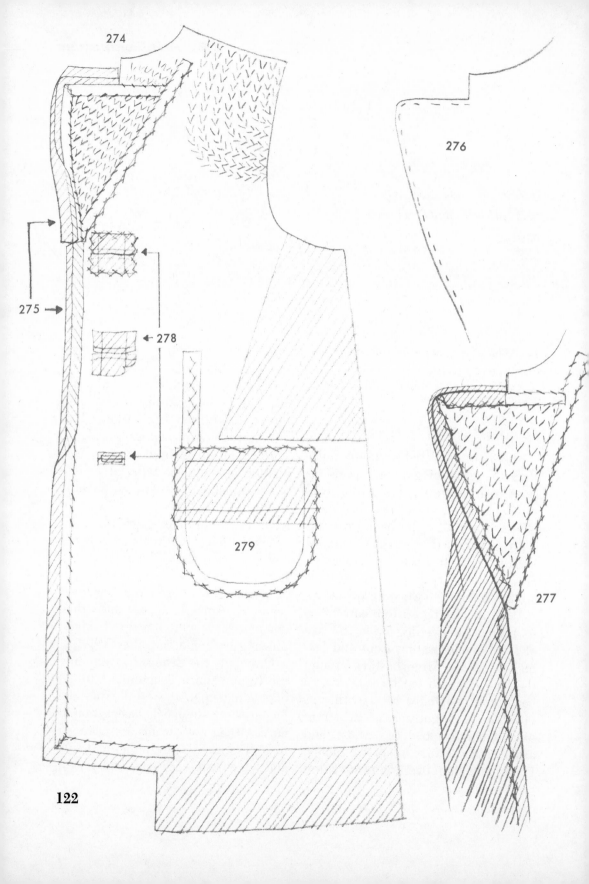

274

276

275 →

← 278

279

277

Turn the front and facing to the right side of garment and crease between the thumb and forefinger for basting.

This is a good place to use up scraps of silk thread (if they are fast colors), because silk does not leave indentation marks in the material after pressing. Edge-baste the front and facing together with small even stitches, pulling the stitches tight enough to hold them firmly together, Fig. 276.

The facing seam margin may be catch-stitched onto the tape of lapel to keep the seam from rolling; then clip the seam margin on front and catch-stitch to facing below lapels, Fig. 277.

At this point, cut small windows in the interfacing the size of the button-hole opening, and pull the buttonhole strips through. Catch-stitch to the interfacing to keep in place, Fig. 278.

If pockets extend under the foundation, slash into foundation and lay pocket on top. Catch-stitch to foundation (do not pick into front material) to keep pocket in place, Fig. 279.

This assures a smooth appearing front on the right side of the garment, and prevents wearing around the finished edges of pocket and buttonhole welts.

Diagonal Basting

Diagonal basting controls the position of seams while the garment is in construction. Place break line of lapel on the edge of table, letting lapel drop over the edge with facing of garment on top. Diagonally baste to the end of break line. Then turn so garment front is on top, roll edge over fingertips and continue diagonal basting down the front and around the corner to where lining is to be attached. Diagonal basting is always done to keep the seam margins curved to the inside of the garment, Fig. 280.

In tailoring, the hands and mind should be trained to hold the material the way it is worn on the body. The seams and edges of the garment

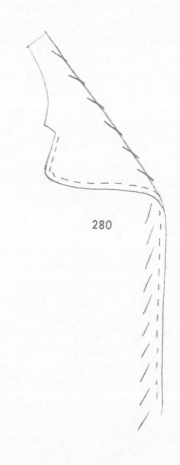

280

should curve in toward the body on all finished sections.

Always smooth lapel fullness toward the sides of a garment when basting and sewing, never ease it toward the shoulder or hemline.

Press edges of fronts on a hard surface with a press cloth until thoroughly steamed, then pound with a block of hardwood to flatten the edges. After removing edge bastings, repeat if necessary.

Joining Front Lining to Facing

Baste the front lining to the facing, easing a little at the bust and making sure the lining is as long as the coat front and not the facing.

Machine stitch lining and facing together with lining facing the feeder of machine, Fig. 281. Machine stitch darts in place, or feather stitch by hand, with lining darts matching garment darts.

Baste them in place until the garment is completed and feather stitch, if finished by hand.

Lay the garment on a table with facing and front as smooth as possible. When smoothing front facing, rub toward side seams, *never up and down.* When basting, keep all fullness over the bustline.

With the facing on top, baste through the front, foundation, and facing where it is stitched to the lining, from hem to 5″ from shoulder. Baste in the facing only, Fig. 282.

Fold the lining back and catch-stitch lining and facing seam margins

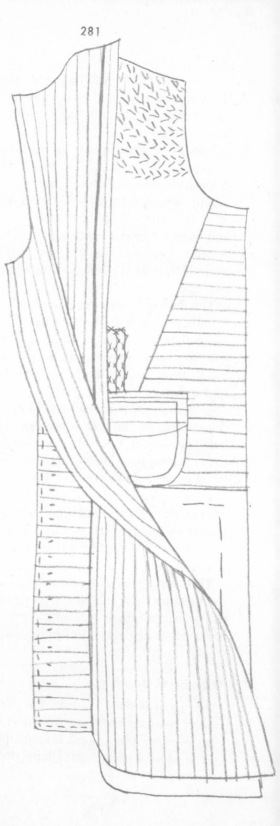

to foundation from 2″ above hem to 5″ from shoulder. Do not catch-stitch into front of garment or into outside part of pocket, Fig. 283.

Lay lining back on top of front, matching seams and darts, if any. Lining seams should be flush with front seams and darts.

Baste about 2″ above the hem across the bottom, up the sides, to armscye, cutting diagonally across the shoulder so there will be room for shoulder pads, Fig. 284.

Trim lining to a scant ¼″ larger than side seam of garment. Trim foundation and lining around armscye and across the shoulder from the right side.

After fronts have been completed with front linings attached, attach a muslin yoke interfacing to the back. If there is a center back seam in the garment, a yoke interfacing may be held in place with a backstitch down this center back seam, Fig. 285. Be sure there is no tension in these stitches, to avoid puckering. Baste side seams together, using the same seam allowance as when garment was fitted. Machine stitch and press open on a seam board. See page 126.

Interface the lower back

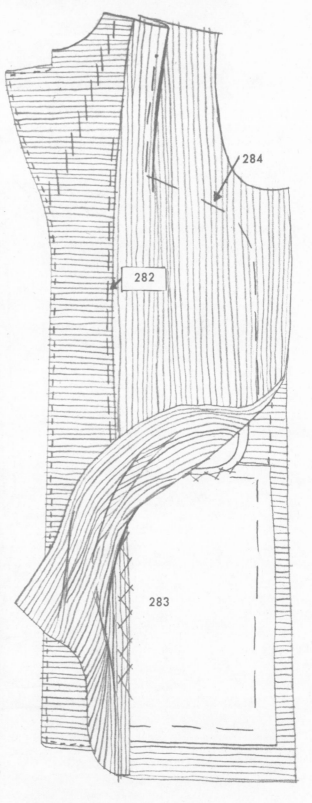

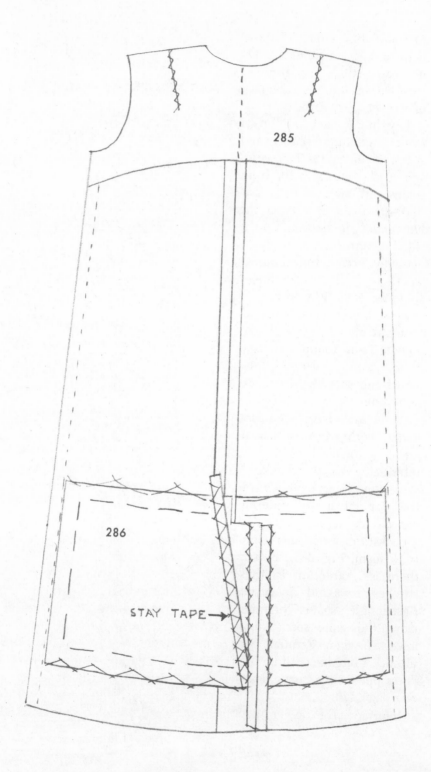

285

286

STAY TAPE→

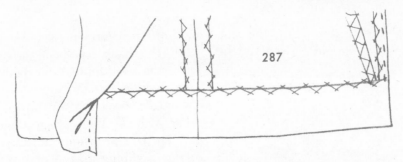

287

section from hemline to 1″ above vent opening, or to waistline, whichever fabric would demand, Fig. 286. (When using loosely woven fabrics, an interfacing reaching to waistline would be desirable for warmth.) For reinforcing vents and pleats with stay-tape, see Reinforced or Split Seams, page 105.

Finishing Hem of Garment

Crease baste the hem even with front facings, using tailor tacks, or chalk mark, as a guide for hem crease.

Baste hem crease in garment with small stitches, using contrasting basting thread. Pin, or baste, the shoulder seams together, insert shoulder pads, and check to see if the hem is even before pressing.

When trying on a garment, be sure to use shoulder pads if they are to be used permanently, and pin the fronts together accurately for each fitting.

If the hem is correct, trim to 1¼″ wide for jackets and 2½″ for coats. Press with a press cloth to shrink out fullness, using vertical strokes, never horizontal. After hem has been permanently pressed, catch-stitch to garment interfacing, or hem interfacing,

being careful not to pick through to outside of fabric, Fig. 287.

When the interfacing does not act as interfacing for the hem, follow instructions for Interfaced Hems, page 51, with the exception of the machine stitching around the extended edge of the interfacing. Because the lining seals this hem, it receives very little strain, and the reinforcement stitching on extended part of interfacing is unnecessary.

Joining Back Sections of Lining to Front

Before joining the back sections of lining to fronts, check to see if there is enough ease for a freedom pleat at the center back. A freedom pleat is a fold placed in the lining to assure ease for both comfort and action. If not, extend lining material 1″ when cutting, or when there is no center seam, move the pattern over to widen the back by 1″. If the lining has 3 sections, join side to center back and press open.

Place the lining on back section of garment, and baste added amount in fold down the center back, but do not baste lining to the back. This is just to check fit. At this point, the side lining sections should be exactly the size of the garment side sections. After the back has been fitted, remove the back lining from back garment section.

Fold front sections on top of each other with the lining on top and the garment turned inside out. Lay back section of lining on top of front sections, with right sides of lining facing each other. Baste lining side seams of

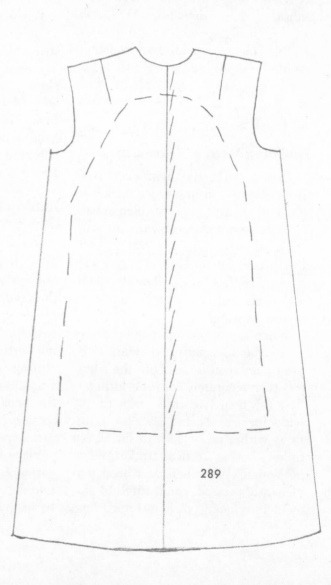

288

289

*"Turn to right side and
trim lining . . ."*

the front and back sections together
and machine stitch.

Press the lining seams open on the
edge of a seam board. Permanently
baste lining and garment side seams
together, using loose 1″ stitches. Always use white cotton thread, starting
with a knot and ending with a knot
2″ from armscye to 3″ from hem. Regardless of garment color, use white
permanent basting thread if it will not
shadow through, Fig. 288.

When the back is in three sections,
move lining shoulder section seam
over to garment shoulder section seam
and repeat the permanent basting
procedure done on side seams of garment and lining. Reach in between
back lining and fronts, grasping the
shoulders and turn inside out. The
lining is now in place. Smooth lining
toward center of back.

Baste about 2″ above hem from
center seam to side, up the back and
diagonally across shoulder to center, as illustrated. Baste from the opposite side to center, laying surplus
lining into center pleat up to neck
and across shoulder. Do not fold
more than 1½″ into lining at center
back, Fig. 289.

Turn to right side and trim lining

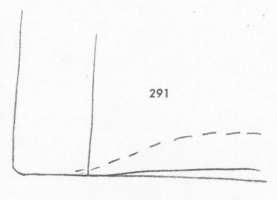

290

even around hem, letting it extend
about 1¼″ longer than garment hem,
Fig. 290.

Turn back to inside of garment and
tuck lining underneath facing. Keep
lining slightly above garment at facing, gradually raising it to ½″ higher
than garment hem across back, Fig.
291.

When basting the lining hem, keep
bastings just below garment hem
finish.

If garment is not too bulky, place it
on your lap to finish the hem. Do not

291

press the lining hem until the hem is finished.

Where the lining is tucked under the facing, use a finishing stitch to fasten firmly for 1", then roll lining fold back to basting line, holding with thumb and forefinger. Use a small running stitch and pick up inside portion of garment hem, then small stitch in lining portion of fold. Keep staggering stitches, first one in the garment hem, then one into lining until the lining is anchored to coat all across the bottom, Fig. 292.

This method of hemming leaves a small pleat, or surplus fold of lining, at the bottom, when completed, to allow for shrinkage when pressed and cleaned.

Darts which have been basted to match with garment darts should be feather-stitched for the final finish.

Closing Shoulders

Baste the outer garment shoulder seams together for permanent fitting, easing the back onto the front,

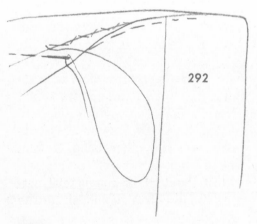

292

whether or not this is mentioned in pattern instructions. Be careful not to sew front interfacing in with shoulder seams, but back yoke interfacing can be sewn in with seams.

After several "try-ons," shrink out fullness, machine stitch, and press seams open on a seam board. When shrinking seam fullness, leave seams together and dampen full side of seam, pressing up and down until flat, just overlapping stitching line.

Neck and Armscye, Reinforced

Starting 1" or 1½" from collar notch, backstitch in outer garment only, just inside stitching line where collar is attached. Proceed across back to 1½" from opposite collar notch. This will stay-stitch neck seams so they will not stretch out of shape.

Silk buttonhole floss, pulled over beeswax, is best to use on neck and armscye. This stitching retains the shape of neck and armscye permanently, and eliminates bulk.

Backstitch ½" from raw edge, or just inside stitching line, around armscye, 1½" from back shoulder seam to 1" or 2" from front shoulder seam. Keep backstitch taut around armscye and at curved area in front. Pull tight enough to give a shirred appearance. Keep stitches easy when crossing underarm seams. Shrink out excessive fullness before inserting sleeve.

QUESTIONS

1. Where is ease placed in a lining? How is the lining machine stitched?

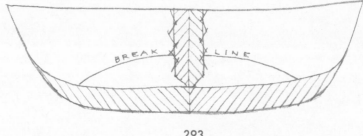

BREAK LINE

293

2. Describe two methods of finishing darts.
3. Explain how lining and garment seams are attached to interfacing.
4. Where are linings basted to fronts?
5. How are muslin yokes attached?
6. Why are backs interfaced from hemline to waist?
7. Where are hems basted for finishing?
8. Describe the finishing of a hem.
9. How are hems treated when interfacing doesn't extend across the back?
10. What is a freedom pleat?
11. How are back lining sections prepared and attached to a garment?
12. How is a lining prepared for final finishing?
13. Are front and back interfacings sewn into shoulder seams?
14. Describe the finishing of shoulder seams.
15. Give the necessary steps in the reinforcement of the neck and armscye.

Preparing and Attaching Notched Collar to Garment

Always cut the undercollar on the bias, with the seam in center back. Baste center back seams, and press open. Cut interfacing of collar from soft raw or elastic collar linen. Do not use haircloth for interfacing collars unless the front of the garment and collar are cut in one piece. When making white, or very light pastel garments, use bleached interfacing fabrics in collars and interfacings.

Baste the undercollar and machine stitch together at center back. Cut interfacing, minus seam allowance, across neck edge and center back, Fig. 293. Baste or pin to coat across front and back of garment neck. Try on the garment and place a chalk mark on the collar interfacing where the lapel breaks. Also, place a chalk mark in the center back crease of the collar where it feels comfortable on the neck for break line.

Every neck is different in size and in length, from shoulder to hair line, and the collar must be fitted accordingly. A person with a short neck requires a short or narrow collar stand, otherwise the collar will creep up into the hair line and feel unnecessarily bulky. On the other hand, a long neck needs a deeper collar stand.

Most standard, or commercial patterns, are usually high enough for the

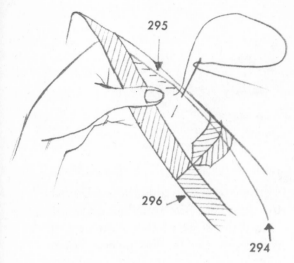

295

296

294

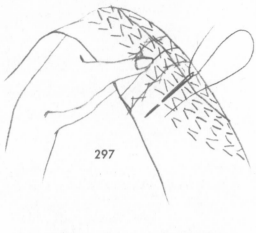

297

person with the longer neck from nape to hair line.

When fitting a collar and lapel, check to be sure that previously marked collar and lapel break lines are correctly placed.

By placing the collar on the lengthwise fold, or on straight grain of material, the outer edges can be shaped and stretched to curve across the shoulders more easily. Never cut the collar parallel to the lengthwise grain.

Remove undercollar from garment and baste interfacing to undercollar. Re-mark crease, or collar break, with chalk as illustrated. Machine stitch together on chalk mark for pad-stitching guide, Fig. 294.

Begin pad-stitching the undercollar and interfacing together on the marked break line, working toward the neck seam, Fig. 295. Use the tailor's padding stitch. See Tailor's Quilting or Padding Stitch, page 22.

After finishing the first row of padding stitches, roll the collar over the 4 fingers of the left hand and brace them on your knee. Hold this roll with the thumb and quilt back and forth until the collar stand is completed, with the exception of seam margin across the back of the neck, Fig. 296.

Do not turn the collar while working, but work parallel padding stitches about ¼" apart until the stand is completely filled in. *Note:* Pad-stitching thread should never be pulled taut.

Turn the collar and work from break line to outside of collar seam allowance, Fig. 297. Quilt the outside, parallel with machine stitching by rolling over the 4 fingers and bracing on the knees, as the inside was done, or quilt up and down from center to each end. Whichever is done, be sure to keep the thread relaxed. If the thread is pulled taut the collar will not shape and roll properly. The safest way for the beginner is to start

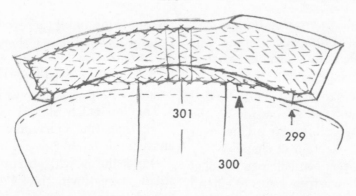

298

301 300 299

quilting in the center of the back and quilt up and down toward each end of the collar. By working in this manner, the stitches will be less apt to become taut.

Finishing Top Collar by Hand

Trim all seam margins of collar interfacing, and all undercollar seam margins to ¼". Crease-baste around undercollar and press. Catch-stitch undercollar seams to interfacing, Fig. 298.

Miter the corners and catch-stitch them together to eliminate bulky corner seams.

Press the seams until they are hard and flat. Dampen collar interfacing thoroughly, and press dry. Dampen neck edge of collar and press across back and over shoulder, stretching slightly. Always press completely dry to retain the shape. Turn to the outside and press and stretch as in previous step.

When the collar is completely dry and stretched to curve over the shoulder and back of neck, fold on the machine stitching and crease with

iron. Do not crease where neck seam is joined to the coat.

Baste top collar, overlapping undercollar slightly, and press. These press marks will be a guide for finishing the collar.

Clip the lapel all the way to stitching, where the collar joins the lapel, if it has not been clipped before, Fig. 299.

Baste unfinished undercollar to garment and try on for a final check to see if everything is in perfect order before finishing. This method can be applied to any style garment with set-on collar. The lapel break should continue into collar break.

Baste the undercollar across the neck from lapel to lapel. Clip facing seam margin 1½" from shoulder seam, the depth of the seam. Turn under and baste facing seam margin from clipped edge to collar notch, Fig. 300. Blend garment and interfacing seams by trimming garment front less than interfacing, from collar notch to shoulder seam. Catch-stitch front and foundation seam margin to the undercollar, continuing across the back of the garment. In crossing back of garment neck, catch-stitch lining and garment back to collar interfacing, Fig. 301. See page 133.

Keep the lapel and collar folded over the hand, as it is worn on the body, while basting. Press lapel over tailor's ham to retain its shape.

Baste, or pin, top collar to finished undercollar, and trim seams to extend approximately ½″ larger than finished undercollar.

Collar and undercollar may be separated for the following step, or they may remain basted together. If separating collar and undercollar is preferred, crease-baste edges of top collar to overlap undercollar. Trim seam margin to ¼″ and press. Catch-stitch seam edge to top collar loosely. Miter corners to eliminate bulk. Be sure the stitching doesn't show on the right side. Press carefully and pound seams.

When the collar and undercollar are kept together for this operation, they should be basted inside the seam margin so that crease-bastings can be removed.

When completing collar before attaching to garment, baste undercollar across back of neck and catch-stitch interfacing and garment front seams from collar notch to shoulder seam, as previously mentioned. Baste top collar butted against facing seam margin and continue across neck of garment. Be sure to hold collar and lapels as they will be worn, to assure needed fullness.

The top collar seam should overlap the garment lining across the back. Before finishing, baste the top collar all around the sides and across the back, slightly overlapping the undercollar to keep seams invisible.

The top collar should be slightly fuller than the undercollar to retain an easy roll.

Hand finish with blind felling stitch, using linen thread or thread pulled across beeswax for strength. It is always easier to finish the top collar if crease-basted and thoroughly pressed before attaching to undercollar.

If the material is bulky, undercollar felt or flannel may be used with a raw edge finish. If the top collar fabric is hard to match in felt or flannel, garment fabric may be used. To control fraying, rub a hot knife on beeswax, and then onto the raw edge of collar. *Note:* Do not use beeswax in excessive amounts; it may leave grease marks. Finish with a buttonhole stitch, catching seam of top collar only.

Finishing Top Collar by Machine

Finish undercollar quilting, or padding, and trim interfacing seam allowance at neck. Catch-stitch undercollar neck seam to interfacing. Do not trim and catch-stitch the other three sides.

Dampen and press the collar on neck portion by stretching in a circular motion. Turn to outside of break line and press and stretch at the same time, where the collar curves across the shoulder seams.

After the collar is pressed thoroughly dry, fold on collar break, or stitching line, and crease with iron across the back of neck and down to neck seam. *Note:* Never crease across the neck seam.

Baste undercollar to garment across the back of neck for a second fitting before sewing the top collar, because pressing stretches the undercollar.

After the undercollar is basted to the garment, place a chalk mark at junction of lapel and collar, as a stitching guide.

Fold undercollar in half and pin together. Trim away excess, leaving ¼" seam margin at the ends and across the back of collar, Fig. 302.

Since the undercollar has been fitted to the garment, fit the top collar to undercollar. Fold the top collar to find the center back. Place center back of top collar on center back of undercollar, right sides facing. Baste from center back, around corner to collar junction by holding the collar over finger for needed ease, with the top collar on top, Fig. 303. Fold ends

of collar together, keeping top and undercollars flush. Then trim collar even with undercollar, Fig. 304. Place open ends of collar together and baste from lapel and collar junction to center back, holding over finger with upper collar on top, Fig. 305.

Shrink the fullness out before sewing by machine, using a tailor's ham.

Start machine stitching where the neck seam has been turned under, keeping ¼" seam all around.

Stitch through interfacing and undercollar where hand finished collars have interfacing trimmed away. Stitch two stitches across corners instead of pivoting on the needle. Trim undercollar and interfacing seam margin to ⅛". Trim both seam margins around the curves to ⅛". Turn collar, roll seams out firmly, and edge baste with small stitches. If material is heavy, place a second row of bastings, to retain roll line.

Press over a tailor's ham with a press cloth. The interfacing in the undercollar helps to keep the seam smooth and acts as flat-stitching. Press the collar over a tailor's ham again to keep the shape, and crease the edges

302

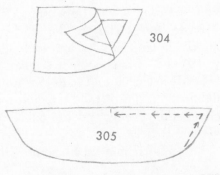

303

304

305

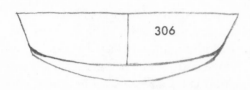

306

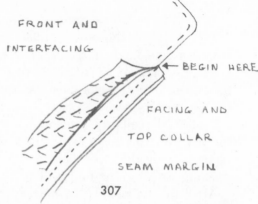

FRONT AND
INTERFACING
← BEGIN HERE
FACING AND
TOP COLLAR
SEAM MARGIN

307

at the same time. Fold top collar over undercollar crease, or break line, and baste on crease with overcasting stitch to keep top collar in place and retain the necessary fullness.

Trim the top collar ¼″ longer than undercollar in front where it is joined to lapels, and graduate to ⅜″ across back of neck, Fig. 306.

Where the top collar is stitched to the facing, the seam margin should be about ¼″ longer than the undercollar seam that has previously been catch-stitched across the neck. Keep seam of top collar and undercollar open about ¼″, or depth of hem.

Place both ends of collar together and chalk mark stitching line so the end of the collars are even when finished.

Place lapels together and mark with chalk where the collar will be attached. Match top collar chalk mark to lapel chalk mark and baste, holding collar on top, curved over the fingers to keep the lapel and collar roll in same position it will be worn.

Baste top collar to lapel, from matched points of lapel and top collar to 1½″ or 2″ from shoulder seam.

Fold coat front and haircloth foundation back out of the way, and machine stitch facing and top collar together.

Lower machine needle into the feeder of machine and butt the lapel up against it before starting to sew the top collar and facing together. Hold bobbin and top threads until the machine begins to stitch. This is important so the collar and lapel will look like one continuous seam. Use a medium, small stitch and sew very straight to 1½″ or 2″ of shoulder seam, or to notch. Leave threads long enough at collar to knot, or thread a needle and tack, Fig. 307.

This seam must have *only one row* of stitching. Tie or tack stitches at the beginning and end of stitching, whether done by hand or machine. When tacking by hand, thread needle with extended machine thread and tack. Then pull needle through material and clip thread.

Press the seam open on the edge of a seam board, dampen with the fingertips and press thoroughly dry. When complete, trim to ¼″ inch seam margin.

Baste the coat front and foundation to the collar seams, letting the facing seam margin fall down inside the garment front after it has been

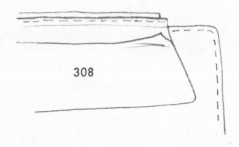

308

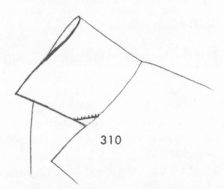

310

trimmed to ¼". This is a permanent basting, and, therefore, needs to be held and sewn the way it will be worn, curved over the hand with collar on top, Fig. 308.

Baste the undercollar one half at a time, across the back of the garment, from the center back to the lapel. Stitch only to back of garment, *not* through lining or top collar.

If there is the least excess of fullness, place about ¼" at each shoulder seam, then shrink away.

Baste back lining over front facing at shoulder seams about ½" at neck. Catch-stitch lining and back of garment to collar linen, in center back. Place excess lining in freedom pleat and baste in center back of garment, Fig. 309.

Fold collar at break line and overcast at collar break to retain needed amount of fullness.

Baste top collar over facing and across back lining where the machine stitching ends.

Press on a tailor's ham and finish with a blind finishing stitch, using linen thread, or thread which has been rubbed with beeswax for strength.

Miter and trim excess seams at the corner where it is joined to facing before hand finishing the back collar.

If the undercollar still appears to be too bulky, cut away corner and buttonhole stitch raw edges instead of felling across the ends of undercollar, Fig. 310.

QUESTIONS

1. On what grain-line are undercollars and interfacings cut?
2. When is hymo used in undercollars?

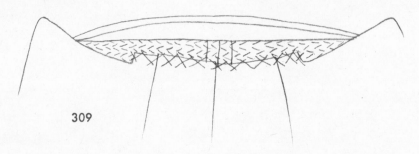

309

3. How do you find the break line in a collar?
4. On what grain line should top collars be cut?
5. Where is the undercollar machine stitched for pad-stitching?
6. Where do you begin pad-stitching the undercollar? How is the collar held?
7. How does the hand-finished undercollar differ from that on the machine stitched collar?
8. Why are collar seams pressed and stretched at the same time?
9. How is the top collar attached?
10. How are the garment seams prepared and attached to the undercollar?
11. How do you hold the top collar when basting to the undercollar?
12. How do you obtain correct seam allowance for the top collar?
13. How should a top collar and undercollar be aligned?
14. How are collars usually finished when made of bulky fabric?
15. How is the neck seam of a collar finished?
16. Do you crease the collar break at neck seam?

17. Why should the undercollar be basted to the garment for fitting after pressing?
18. After the undercollar has been fitted, how do you prepare it for joining to the top collar?
19. Describe steps involved in joining the top collar and undercollar.
20. How do we match lapels and collar notches, for finishing?
21. Where should excess fullness be placed?
22. How are corners treated to avoid a bulky appearance?

Construction of Shawl or Roll Collar—Garment and Collar in One Piece

Baste together and fit carefully for try-ons, and determine collar break line before sewing by machine.

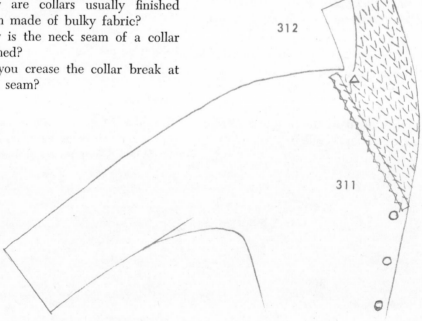

312

311

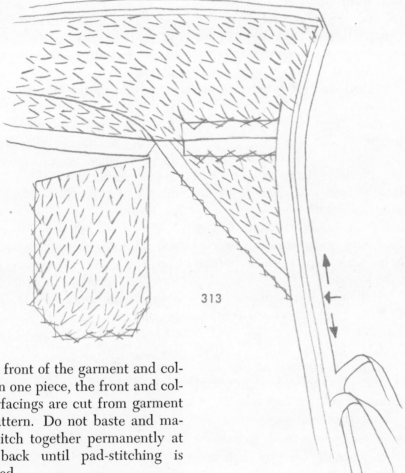

313

If the front of the garment and collar are in one piece, the front and collar interfacings are cut from garment front pattern. Do not baste and machine stitch together permanently at center back until pad-stitching is completed.

Mark and baste interfacings to front at lapel and collar break lines, Fig. 311. Pad-stitch as previously indicated, continuing across back of collar, being careful not to cross break line. Stop at center back seam line, Fig. 312. Shape fronts, attach tape, and continue closing up facing to within 1½″ of center back seam. After right and left fronts have been joined together, catch-stitch center lapel seam margins to interfacing, then pad-stitch the half-moon area of collar. Machine stitch center back seam, and press open.

Baste facing to front from center back of neck to hemline, easing small amount of fullness over pad-stitched area.

Press front and facing seams open. Trim front seam margin to slightly over ⅛″. Trim facing seam margin to a little more than ¼″. Edge-baste fronts, continuing around collar, using small basting stitches. Catch-stitch the front seam margin to the facing, around collar. Clip seam to stitching line, and catch-stitch to facing below collar, Fig. 313. Baste second row of diagonal basting from top button to hemline.

Place break line of lapel on edge of table with lapel hanging over, and diagonally baste in place to retain fullness.

Join front lining to front facing. Baste facing and front together to keep in place, easing extra fullness over the bust area.

Carefully smooth toward side seams while basting, never toward hemline or shoulder.

Catch-stitch seam margins of front and facings to foundation of garment, as in previous instructions. Cut windows in hymo for buttonholes before closing fronts of garment.

Before joining sides and back seams together, place the back on table and carefully smooth out and fit back lining to garment back.

If the back has one center seam, leave a 1″ fold for a pleat in center. Baste the pleat into lining but do not baste to garment after lining has been fitted. If the lining is larger than back, pin or baste, and trim to the exact size of garment back, including pleat.

If the back has three sections, the side seams of the lining and garment back should be flush with each other

and the pleat in the center back panel. Trim this lining to fit. Reinforce the neck inside the stitching line, with buttonhole twist, regardless of collar style.

Before closing shoulders permanently be sure the back of garment does not have to be raised. Join side and back seams together. Press seams open on edge, or seam board. Fold the insides of fronts on top of each other with right sides of lining on top, as illustrated.

Place back lining on top with right side of lining facing. Baste side and shoulder seams of front and back linings and machine stitch, Fig. 314. Press seams open, and stay baste lining and garment seams together about 3″ from bottom and top. Using white basting thread, stay baste, keeping stitches about 1″ apart. Place lining seams facing garment seam while stay basting together.

Turn lining and garment right side out by reaching between back lining and front, grasping the shoulders of garment and pulling toward the body.

Baste lining to garment back, starting about 2″ from armscye, angling up toward center of back to leave room for inserting shoulder pads.

Baste across the bottom of garment about 4″ from hemline to keep the lining intact while turning up the hem in coat or jacket.

After the garment is hemmed (see Hems, page 48), tuck the lining under the edge of the facing at the hem and baste ½″ from the crease of lining

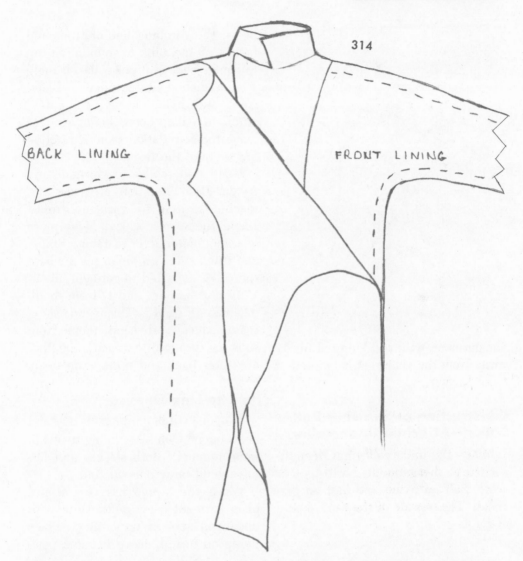

BACK LINING   314   FRONT LINING

hem. Gradually raise the lining about ½″ above the crease of the garment hem across the fronts and back so it will not stretch and hang below the garment hem when garment is completed. Always finish lining hem near the finished edge of garment hem.

Whip lining firmly to hem where the lining is attached to facing, for 1″.

Fold the lining back to basting and continue with felling stitch by taking small stitch into the garment hem, then up into the lining. Stagger the stitches, first into the garment, then into the lining hem. Catch into single fold of garment and lining hem so stitches do not show on right sides.

When there is a vent, or pleat, in

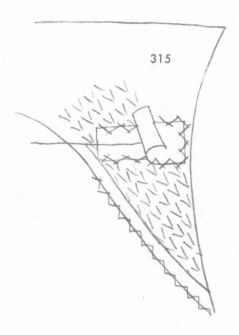

315

be on the stitching line of front and facing. Whip tape to foundation, up to center back seam of collar, leaving 1″ unattached at that point. Blend front and hymo seams and catch-stitch to collar linen, being sure to leave the foundation seam a fraction longer than the front.

Baste undercollar to garment and try on. If no alterations are necessary, machine stitch to garment fronts. Blend the seams. Cut 1″ bias piece of wigan material, or matching lining, and catch-stitch on top of seam where the collar is basted to garment, about ½″ from front edge and 1″ from shoulder seam, Fig. 315. This is to cushion seam edges and keep them from showing through. Join facing together at center back and press seam open.

the garment, whip the lining firmly 1″ away from the vent as it is finished at front facings.

Construction of Shawl or Roll Collar—Attached Undercollar

When the undercollar has been attached to the garment, baste tape to front, half on hymo and half on garment. The outside of the tape should

How to Line Sleeves

Machine stitch garment sleeves and press open. Complete lining seams in same manner. Both sleeves and lining should be wrong side out.

When the sleeve has two seams, place garment sleeve on the table with underarm section uppermost. Place lining on top of sleeve in same posi-

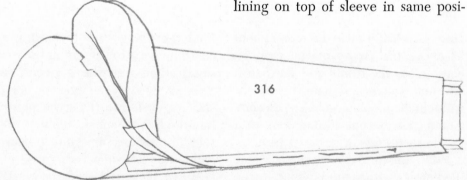

316

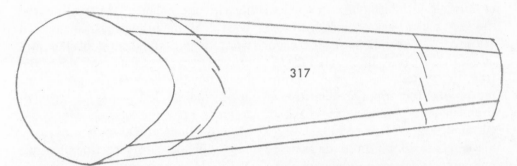

317

tion so that underarm sections of lining and sleeves match.

When the sleeve has only one seam, place lining seam and garment seam facing each other so that notches match.

Raise the lining about ⅛" above the sleeve. Stay-baste the lining seam, or seams, together, depending upon the style, 2½" from the top to 3 or 4 inches from hem, Fig. 316. Reach inside top sleeve and turn to right side. Baste around sleeve about 2½" below top of armscye, and about 5" from bottom to hold lining and sleeve together temporarily, Fig. 317.

Sewing in Sleeves

Try on jacket with shoulder pads to check collar fit before sewing in sleeves. Be sure to check for body wrinkles under arms, and across the back. If the garment front, across the chest at armscye, bulges considerably, gradually trim armscye, starting 3" below shoulder seam to the point where curve under the armpit begins. Gradually trim to ¼" at point of curve and decrease to nothing again, Fig. 318. This trimming away of seam

eliminates unsightly bulge and an uncomfortable feeling when you wear the garment.

Too wide a shoulder is more uncomfortable than too narrow a shoulder. At this point, if the shoulder seam is too wide, trim so that the stitching line of the seam will be exactly on top of the ball and socket of the shoulder. This spot can be easily located by placing the opposite hand on the shoulder and pivoting the arm in a circular motion.

Reinforcing Armscye Seam

Rub silk buttonhole twist over beeswax to strengthen and keep it from

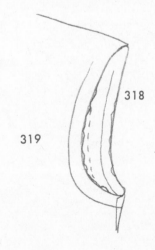

318

319

curling. Fold interfacing back out of the way when backstitching garment armscye. Backstitch in seam margin close to stitching line, starting 1½" from the shoulder seam, and continuing around the armscye seam to 1½" from shoulder seam at the back of garment, Fig. 319, page 143.

Keep backstitch firm so the armscye will not stretch and break machine stitching when the garment is finished. Shirr slightly around curved area in front, then shrink away by dampening seam allowance and pressing with a medium warm iron, using horizontal strokes.

Be sure to place tailor tacks for center underarm guide marks in the sleeve and garment.

Match underarm and overarm marks by pinning together before basting into garment.

Measure the sleeve and garment armscye for fullness. There must be at least 2½" of fullness in the sleeve or

it will not balance properly on the body. More fullness is needed in front, where the leader of the arm crosses over into the chest, than in the back, but the sleeve must not be taut at any point. If there is not enough fullness, raise the sleeve seam about ½" above the garment underarm seam. This will increase the circumference of the sleeve opening.

Start basting the sleeve into garment at center underarm by looking into the sleeve and keeping sleeve and garment curved over the fingers while working, Fig. 320. The sleeve seam must be on top for easing.

While basting the back of sleeves, keep the seams even except where the sleeve has been raised under the arm. At this point, the sleeve will be above the garment. About 1½" from the shoulder seam take ¼" seam on the sleeve seam and retain ½" or ⅝" seam allowance in garment, depending upon the width of seam allowance being used. Continue basting down the front with a ¼" seam on sleeve and ½" or ⅝" on garment to where sleeve starts to curve under the armscye. It

320

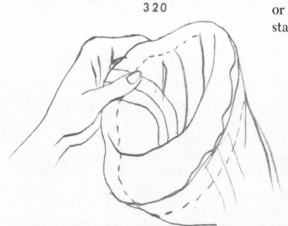

"Start basting the sleeve into garment at center underarm . . ."

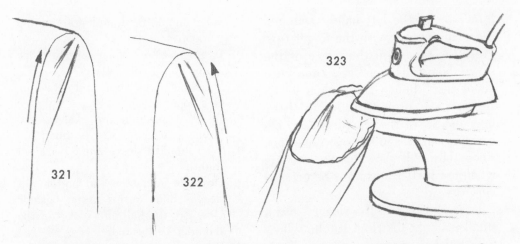

is necessary to have a little more full-ness in the front of sleeves than in the back, but the sleeve should not be tighter than the garment at any point.

In some cases, where the sleeve is extremely tight, offset the underarm mark ¼″ toward the front of garment underarm mark. This will allow more fullness in front, where it is needed. This creates more fullness in the sleeve and the correct pitch is obtained as well as more room for pads and welts. If the sleeve is too full, when basting, a larger seam allowance may be taken, thus reducing the fullness.

There should be enough fullness eased into the sleeve to form a soft fold in front, where leader crosses into the chest. The sleeve should balance by draping slightly over the pocket when the arm is relaxed.

Try on garment with shoulder pads to check the pitch of sleeves, before machine stitching. The cross of basting thread in the upper part of the sleeve will help in balancing the

sleeve. If diagonal folds appear in the sleeve, it is too tight, or the fullness is not properly distributed.

If the bias wrinkles in the sleeve drape from the shoulder toward the front, place more ease in front, taking a deeper seam on the sleeve, under the arm, if necessary, and then easing all the fullness toward the shoulder line, Fig. 321. If wrinkles appear from the shoulder toward back underarm, ease fullness up over the shoulder toward front of garment. Fig. 322.

If a person is extremely sway-backed, swing the center of top sleeve about ½″ from shoulder seam toward front of garment.

After the sleeves are basted correctly, shrink out seam fullness, before machine stitching. Hold the garment and sleeve seam margins together (do not separate seams) cupped over the end of the sleeve board, or the small end of the ironing board, with the sleeve seam uppermost, Fig. 323. Hold the seam margins in place with the thumb and forefinger of the left hand. Dampen the seam margin with the finger tips. Press the seams on the curve of the sleeve board about 2″ at a time until all of the fullness is shrunken away. Be careful to press with the tip of the iron just across the stitching line. Do not press creases in the seam margins, since they will show on the outside when finished. Seams must be pressed very dry and smooth.

When basting in the sleeves, use a small straight basting stitch, which will make it easier to shrink fullness away.

Start machine stitching at the center underarm with the sleeve on top. Machine stitch with medium small stitches, keeping the seam straight while sewing around the sleeve. If the seams are crooked and dip in and out, they will create a scalloped look at the shoulder on right side of the garment.

Re-shrink the sleeve seams after machine stitching, before inserting the pads. When garment has extended shoulder line and set-in sleeve, press sleeve and garment seams open, or apart. This is a combination drop shoulder and set-in sleeve style.

QUESTIONS

1. How do shawl, or roll collars, differ from set-on collars, in construction?
2. When are fronts of garment and collar joined together at center back?
3. Where do you start basting facings to fronts?
4. How are front linings attached?
5. What should be done before joining garment side seams?
6. Is it necessary to reinforce neck seams on all collar styles?
7. Describe preparation and attaching of a separate undercollar.
8. In what position are sleeves and linings placed for stay-basting?
9. Why should a sleeve lining be raised slightly?
10. How far from tape and bottoms of sleeves should seams be stay-basted?
11. How can the ball and socket of the shoulder be located?
12. Where do you place a reinforcing stitch around the armscye? Where do you shirr?
13. Where do you place tailor tack guide marks?
14. How much fullness is needed to ease a sleeve properly?
15. Where do you begin basting a sleeve into the armscye?
16. How should a sleeve be held when basting?
17. How do the front sleeve seams differ from the back seams?
18. Where is the most fullness needed in a sleeve seam?
19. What is a helpful guide in getting the correct balance of sleeve?
20. What steps can be taken to eliminate bias wrinkles in the sleeve?
21. At what point and how do you shrink out fullness in seams?
22. How do you treat seams in extended shoulder and sleeve seams?

Inserting Shoulder Pads in Set-in Sleeves

Fold lining back out of the way at shoulder seam, or armscye. Place the left hand inside garment and hold

146

foundation in place, or pin to shoulder and sleeve seam. Smooth into place from the outside toward the armscye with the right hand. Baste the interfacing, or foundation, to garment front from the right side around armscye. Place bastings about 1" from shoulder seam and down the front at armscye.

Sponge rubber pads covered with felt should be used because they are more durable than other pads. Never use foam rubber pads for permanent padding, unless they can be dry-cleaned. When using commercial pads, squared off on one side, the square side goes to the front. If the pad is shaped alike at each side, it may be used either way. Pads on which the sleeve seam edge is cut straight, and unfinished, are for use with set-in sleeves. Pads which have sloped, finished sleeve seam edges, are for dolman, raglan, or curved shoulder lines.

Place the pad between *interfacing* and *lining*. Fold in half and place

center on shoulder seam inside the garment. Extend the pad out into the sleeve at least ½" at the shoulder seam. Place 2 pins about 1" below the shoulder seam in front. Pin the lower outer points of pad to sleeve seam at stitching line in front and back of garment. Do all fitting of pads from the right side of garment, with garment draped over left hand.

Check to see that the garment is smooth from the point of pad at sleeve seam to shoulder seam in the front, and back. If there is any fullness, remove the pins below the shoulder seam in front and ease pad out into the sleeve, until the garment and pad are smooth. The pad may be moved out as much as 1½" if necessary. After doing this, replace pins in front below the shoulder seam.

The foundation is never machine stitched to the garment. Baste pad firmly to coat around armscye, catching all the way through to pad and foundation, Figs. 324 and 325. Tack pad firmly in front and back at sleeve

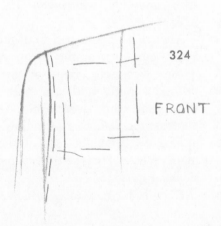

324

FRONT

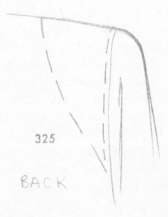

325

BACK

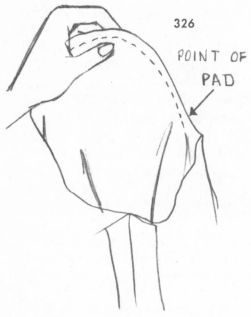

326

POINT OF
PAD

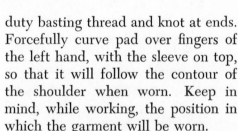

327

seam before trimming. Keep seam margins out into the sleeve when basting the pad in place, and be careful not to catch the lining. Turn to inside of garment.

Trim the pad and seam margins from ¼" to ½" across the shoulder seams, back to ¼" at end of pad. Be sure the pads are trimmed to a razor smooth finish. If material is very heavy, blend the seams, keeping upper seam longer, which will avoid a ragged looking seam from the right side. Recheck to be sure edges of pad look smooth from the right side of the garment when pads are attached, and that both shoulders are trimmed equally. The points of pads should be even with stitching where the sleeves are sewn into the garment, Fig. 326.

Thread several needles with double

duty basting thread and knot at ends. Forcefully curve pad over fingers of the left hand, with the sleeve on top, so that it will follow the contour of the shoulder when worn. Keep in mind, while working, the position in which the garment will be worn.

Tack pad to sleeve and garment seam margin, barely catching points of pad over sleeve stitching. Catch foundation in this step. Overcast pad and seam margin firmly, but not tightly, all the way to stitching line. If ragged edges appear on the pad, trim smoothly while working, Fig. 327.

Always keep the pad and garment firmly curved over the hand, as it is worn. Keep the filler of the pad pushed slightly underneath the garment seam while overcasting. Do not overcast too firmly or a small fold will appear on the right side of the garment when finished, making the sleeve appear too full.

If pads have square corners, trim,

148

rounding off corners. Catch-stitch to foundation from shoulder seam to armscye in the front only, being sure the pad lies smoothly against the foundation. When there is a muslin yoke interfacing at the back of garment, catch-stitch pad to it. If not, just catch-stitch to shoulder dart, being sure not to catch the garment, Fig. 328. With matching thread, backstitch pad to garment through shoulder seam from the outside of garment, keeping the long stitch on the inside and the short stitch on the outside. Do not have tension on thread so stitches will be invisible.

How to Make Cotton Sleeve Welts

Sleeve welts are used only in set-in sleeves. Cut a piece of cotton sheet wadding, single thickness, about 4″ wide and as long as the shoulder pad. Cotton sheet wadding may be purchased in folded sheets approximately 12″ x 30″. This is a specially prepared cotton for tailoring purposes, not to be confused with quilting cotton.

Fold 1″ deep the entire length of the cotton strip. Baste with small, even, running basting stitches on the raw edge of fold.

Fold on basting thread from first hem turn to form another 1″ fold. Place a second row of basting to hold in place on edge of this fold, Fig. 329. Cotton wadding is fragile and must be handled with care.

How to Insert Cotton Sleeve Welt

Turn to inside of garment and place the smooth side of cotton welt on top of sleeve seam margins so the welt will drop down into the sleeve when finished, and cushion armscye seams and pads at the same time.

Whip welt to pad and sleeve seam margins just outside machine stitching, by catching into thread in crease

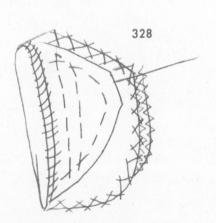

328

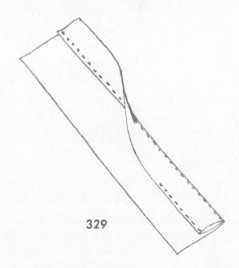

329

of sleeve welt, Fig. 330. Let the single part of welt hang free in the sleeve.

In the front only, fold the welt around the seam about 1½" and overcast to the seam margin, Fig. 331. This welt cushions the rough edge of the pad.

How to Finish Lining

Use silk or linen thread for finishing the lining because it has more elasticity than cotton thread. If using mercerized thread, pull across beeswax to strengthen, and to keep from tangling.

If there is a dart in the front section of lining, baste it in place before proceeding with the following step. The back lining always finishes over front at shoulder seam. Fold back

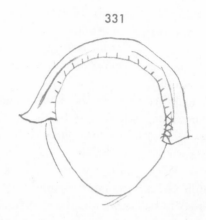

331

lining of garment over front so lining seam will match shoulder seam of garment, Fig. 332.

Check lining at underarm section of garment to be sure it is not too taut, before doing permanent armscye basting. Using heavy white basting thread, baste from inside the sleeve, just outside the stitching line

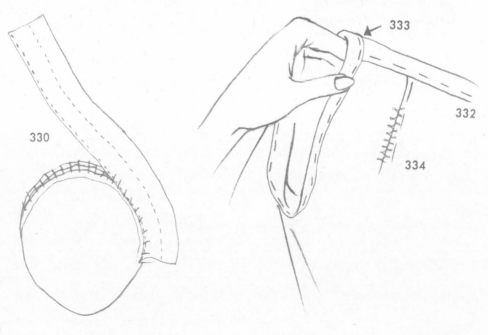

330

333

332

334

in seam margin of sleeve, garment, and garment lining.

If the interfacing extends into the seam margin, baste through it. Baste from underarm seam, around armscye to shoulder pad. At this point bring the needle through seam margin and baste around armscye from the garment lining side, basting lining to pad at stitching line, the full length of the pad. Then bring needle through to inside of sleeve, once more, and continue basting to center underarm seam, close to machine stitching.

This is a permanent basting, and has a dual purpose: It holds the lining and garment together and acts as a marker to which the sleeve lining is hand-finished. When putting in this permanent basting be sure the lining is not pulled too tightly across the chest and back of garment. The lining should always have a little more fullness than the garment. Also, be sure to keep the sleeve welt hanging free into the sleeve. When basting is completed, trim underarm seam to ¼″ from one point of pad to the other.

Place a small chalk mark on front and back lining at the sleeve seams. *Note:* Regardless of style and number of seams, the lining and sleeve seams must be matched. Pin the sleeve lining seams on the chalk mark so the seams of the sleeve and sleeve linings are aligned when sewing into the garment.

Place the fingers of the left hand inside the sleeve and fold under seam allowance of sleeve lining. Let cotton sleeve welt hang free into sleeve between sleeve and lining. Hold sleeve lining on top, with the garment cupped over the fingers, baste sleeve lining to garment and garment lining, slightly overlapping permanent basting, from center underarm seam, around armscye. Fig. 333. By working with sleeve lining in this position, the fullness of the lining automatically eases into place around the armscye. *Remember:* The lining should not be too tight at any point. It is better to have a wrinkle in the lining than in the outer garment.

Finish the lining with a blind finishing stitch. Start at neck and work across the shoulder seam, catching into the pad in a few places to hold the lining in position; then continue around the armscye. Hand-fell sleeve lining to pad while working over pad, but catch into garment lining *only*, under the arm, covering outline basting permanently as you work.

Featherstitch a section of the dart in front lining, about 2″ long, 1″ below shoulder seams, to hold dart in position, Fig. 334, page 150.

Featherstitch 2″ sections of the fold in center back of the lining at neck, waist, and hemline. Other hand-finished darts should also be stitched in this manner.

QUESTIONS

1. Where should shoulder pads be placed in a garment?
2. What type of pads are recommended?

3. Are pads fitted from the right or wrong side of a garment?
4. What focal points do you check for fitting pads?
5. Is a foundation ever machine stitched to a garment?
6. How are pads trimmed?
7. What rule in tailoring should be followed when holding pads and attaching to a garment?
8. What happens when pads are overcast too firmly?
9. Where are cotton sleeve welts used? Why?
10. How are they attached to the armscye seam?
11. Where are they overcast to the seam allowance?
12. What thread is recommended for finishing a lining?
13. What standard procedure should be followed when finishing a lining at the shoulder seams?
14. Where should permanent armscye basting be placed? What is its function?
15. What steps are necessary when basting sleeve linings in garments?
16. In what position do you hold a garment and sleeve while basting together?
17. What stitch is used in finishing a lining?
18. How are darts finished?

Construction of Dolman or Raglan Styles

All styles of garments must be basted and carefully fitted before sewing. Whether the garment has a shawl or attached collar, it is constructed in the same manner.

Dolman Sleeves

Finish the front completely, making buttonholes, pockets, darts, and interfacings. Attach front linings to complete front sections, as in previous instructions.

When collar and garment are cut as one unit, join the back section to front sections across the back of the neck and down the shoulder to end of sleeve.

Press the shoulder seams open and permanently stay-baste the foundation across the shoulder to sleeve seam.

Join facing together at center back and press seams open. Baste facings to the front, easing small amount of fullness around the lapels. Shrink out fullness and machine stitch stay-tape, front, and facing together in one operation. See Construction of Shawl or Roll Collar, page 142.

Complete front lining as previously instructed, but baste sleeve and lining together.

Baste garment together under the arms and fit the shoulder pads in place. This style of garment requires drop shoulder pads. Off shoulder, or drop shoulder pads, are curved over the shoulder cap instead of being squared. The curve of the pad should fit the curve of the shoulder. If the pads feel comfortable and appear properly placed, center them on the shoulder seams and pin in place. Backstitch from the right side of the garment shoulder seam, picking into the shoulder pad, with thread which matches the garment. Keep the small stitches on the top side and the long stitches underneath. Catch-stitch the front of pad to the hymo foundation on the inside front of garment. If there is a seam or gusset near the back of pad, catch-stitch point of pad loosely to seam allowance to keep stitches invisible. If there are no seams in the back, barely pick into the wrong side of the garment back and catch-stitch very loosely to corner of pad. To avoid stitching into the garment back, a muslin yoke interlining may be sewn into garment seams, across the back, during construction.

Be sure the back lining fits the garment back. Baste a freedom pleat into the lining, but do not baste the lining to garment.

Machine stitch the fronts and backs of garment together, under the arms, and down the sides. Press seams open and reinforce at the underarm curve. Fold the fronts on top of each other with the lining side up. Baste the back lining on top with the right sides of the lining facing each other. Machine stitch the back and front *linings* together at the shoulder and side seams.

Press seams open and stay-baste the lining and garment shoulder seams together from shoulder pad to 5″ from the sleeve hem. Stay-baste the underarm seams together 5″ from the sleeve hem to 5″ from the garment hem. Reach between the lining into the sleeves and turn the

sleeves right side out and the lining will be in place. When sleeves and garment are cut in one piece, such as raglan or kimono sleeve, be sure to reinforce underarms with tape around the curved area.

Hand-finish hem and lining according to previous instructions.

Raglan Sleeves

Raglan sleeve styles are finished in the same manner as dolman and kimono sleeves except that the front sleeve sections are joined to the garment front sections, and back sleeves are joined to the garment back sections, before the shoulder seam is sewn. From this point, construct garment—attaching collar, inserting pads, etc.—following instructions for dolman sleeves.

Dolman or Raglan Style with Attached Collar

When the garment has an attached collar, complete the front by joining to front sleeve section. Complete front sections. Join back and back sleeve sections. Join backs and fronts together and complete the garment. Make collar and attach to garment.

How to Measure Sleeve Length

Try on the garment and pin together at center front. Have someone measure the sleeve length, but you can use a mirror to determine the correct length, if no one is available. Turn the hem up slightly below the bend of the wrist, having the outside

153

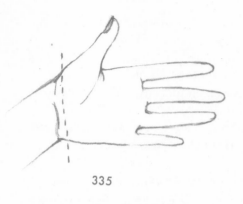

335

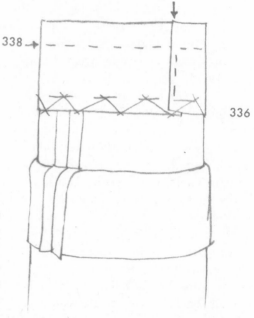

337

338 →

336

of the sleeve a little longer than the underside, Fig. 335. Do not turn up more than 2½″ for sleeve hem.

Measure each sleeve separately because both arms do not measure the same in width or length. Always finish sleeve hems after insertion in garment for a more accurate sleeve length, because of differences in muscular development and variances in style of garments. This is especially true with full length sleeves.

Finishing Sleeve

After sleeve length has been determined, crease baste hem and try on again to check the sleeve length. Cut a bias piece of wigan, or muslin, a little wider than the depth of the sleeve hem. Turn sleeve wrong side out and press on crease basting, with vertical ironing strokes. This also shrinks out the fullness in the sleeve hem.

Remove hem bastings immediately and repress to eliminate thread marks. Catch-stitch bias wigan with large stitches at the crease of sleeve hem, Fig. 336, by overlapping raw edges of interfacing, not forming a seam, Fig. 337.

Machine stitch, or permanently baste, the top of hem to bias piece, Fig. 338. Fold hem up into sleeve. Be sure that hem seam and sleeve seam meet and match. This assures a perfectly smooth finished hem in the completed sleeve of garment. Catch-stitch extended portion of sleeve hem interfacing to sleeve seams. When there is only one seam in a sleeve, put one loose catch-stitch on top of sleeve and interfacing. Do not catch-stitch interfacing to sleeve hem except at these two points. Fell to sleeve hem, but do not catch-stitch

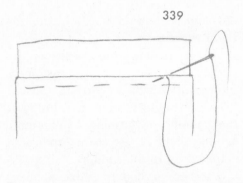

339

through to outside of sleeve. There should be no ease in sleeve lining as there would be in the garment hem. Fell lining firmly to sleeve hem, Fig. 339. All hand-finishing on a garment should be done at one time, such as lining hems, buttonholes, and collar seams.

Final Pressing

The garment should be pressed at this point. Press basted edges, using a dampened press cloth. Remove bastings and press cloth and pound edges with a pounding block for a razor-sharp finish. Remove all bastings except catch-stitching in pockets and buttonholes, and have garment professionally pressed. The pocket and buttonhole bastings may remain until the garment is ready to be worn.

Finishing Bound Buttonholes

See how to make Bound Buttonholes, page 52, before cutting through facing.

After the final pressing, mark buttonholes carefully with basting thread before hand-working, or machine finishing. *Remember:* "Ladies' on the *right* front and gents on the *left* front."

Repress with a damp press cloth to remove thread marks. Use a pounding block and steam and press cloth as often as necessary to give crisp, sharp edges and seams. Some fabrics require two press cloths to avoid marring or felting fabric. Dampen the one next to the garment, placing the dry one on top. Do not press with intense heat—lift iron often. Fabrics with high pile, such as fleeces, coating, sheer worsted, silks, and wool blends, require the second cloth.

Sewing on Buttons

When measuring for button placement, lay the two fronts together with linings facing each other. In ladies' garments, place right front section a fraction longer than left section—in men's do the reverse. With chalk, mark through buttonholes on lower facing in corner of buttonhole closest to side seam, or directly on center front. (If the outside corner of the buttonhole is used, there will not be enough lap to properly close coat fronts.)

QUESTIONS

1. What is the first step in constructing dolman sleeve styles?
2. When is the facing attached?
3. How are dolman style garments completed?
4. What type of shoulder pads are

used? How are they attached at the back of garment?

5. What step is necessary on an underarm seam?
6. Are dolman sleeve linings attached differently than set-in linings?
7. Is raglan sleeve and garment construction different from dolman styles? Why?
8. Explain the difference in construction of dolman, or raglan styles, with attached or unattached collars.
9. How can correct sleeve lengths be ascertained?
10. How can you obtain an accurate guide for finishing a sleeve hem?
11. What is used to interface sleeve hems?
12. How do you attach an interfacing to a hem turn and hem of sleeve?
13. When is the lining attached to a sleeve hem?
14. How should edges of a garment be pressed?
15. What sections remain catch-stitched?
16. Is it necessary to press sections more than once?
17. When should two press cloths be used?
18. How do you find correct placement of buttons on ladies' garments; on men's?

Garment Interlining

When interlining a coat for warmth, the problem is to eliminate bulk and yet retain warmth.

There are various methods of interlining. One is to cut away all seam margins and catch-stitch the interlining to the stitching line of the lining on all sides.

When darts are large, cut away excess and overlap darts, catch-stitching them together.

When joining lining seams together, stitch as close as possible to interlining but *not* into it. Always trim interlining shorter than lining at the hemline of garment to eliminate a bulky hem. Press seams open and catch-stitch to interlining.

Another method is to baste lining and interlining sections together and machine stitch. Blend, or stagger, the seams to eliminate as much bulk as possible. When using heavy interlining, press seams and catch-stitch seam margin to interlining to keep in place. This is more bulky than the previous method, but is more commonly used.

Some lining fabrics have fleece woven on the back for warmth and easy handling. This lining eliminates the interlining and has proved to be very effective both for warmth and smooth lines.

QUESTIONS

1. What problems are encountered when interlining coats?
2. Give two methods of attaching interlinings.

Zip-in Linings

Garments with zip-in linings may be fully lined or may have a half-lining in the front and back, with the garment sleeves fully lined. A fully-lined garment with zip-in lining would be the warmer of the two. Climatic conditions should determine which type of garment is needed.

A removable lining may be made of flannel or any warm material. It may also be made of wool felt, lambs wool, suede, and similar fabrics, and may be lined with silk to seal in seams and feel more comfortable.

Slide fasteners longer than standard length must be custom made, or may be purchased in luggage or tailoring supply stores. All zip-in lined coats must have a facing, across the back of the neck, to which to zip the removable lining. The facing edge must be bound from the hemline all around the neck and down the other side, with bias tape. Baste one-half of the slide fastener tape about 6″ from the hem of garment and ¾″ underneath the inside edge of the facing. This makes the slide fastener invisible.

When making a half-lined garment with zip-in lining, the front lining should cover the front pockets. The garment should be completed and seams below the half-lining must be bound with bias tape.

If the garment is fully lined, baste the tape between the lining and facing. Machine stitch lining and tape in one operation. Press lining seam margin open and finish the garment according to instructions for style being made.

Cut the zip-in lining from the coat lining pattern, but shorter, so that it will barely overlap the coat hem when finished.

When lining a zip-in lining, sew shoulder seams of lining and zip-in lining separately. Baste one-half of the slide fastener tape to the zip-in lining and machine stitch the full length of fastener. Baste lining and zip-in lining together, matching shoulder seams, starting at base of slide fastener, and continuing around the neck and back, down to the opposite end of fastener. Machine stitch lining to slide fastener and zip-in lining, by stitching on previous stitching line. Turn, so that wrong sides of lining and zip-in lining are facing, and flat-stitch edge of zip-in lining as close to slide fastener tape as possible. Place a second row of stitching ¼″ away to keep the fabric from catching in the fastener. Baste and machine stitch side seams of zip-in lining. *Do not catch lining.* Overlap fronts of zip-in lining, with lining portion uppermost. Place back lining on top of front lining with right sides facing; baste and machine stitch side seams.

Press seams open and permanently stay-baste. Any type of hem desired may be used, or lining may be trimmed to crease of hem and zip-in lining turned over it and top-stitched.

When eliminating sleeves in a zip-in lining, scoop armscye approximately ½″ deeper, tuck the two edges in and edge-baste. They may be edge-stitched by machine or hand-felled together with waxed thread. When zip-in lining is unlined, it is advisable to bind seam edge.

Knitted wristlets, either purchased

or hand-knit, may be sewn onto the zip-in lining sleeve for warmth.

When lining the sleeve of a zip-in lining, join seams separately and press open. Turn sleeve right side out, slip wristlet over sleeve and stretch knitted band to ease sleeve fullness into wristlet, and baste together.

Turn lining wrong side out. Slip zip-in lining sleeve and wristlet inside lining sleeve, matching seams. Baste lining and zip-in lining together, with wristlet between them. Machine stitch together with strong thread, stretching wristlet while sewing. Turn sleeve linings right side out, so the raw seams will be enclosed between linings. Stay-baste sleeve seams together.

Baste zip-in sleeve and lining together 2″ from top. Baste zip-in linings together around armscye. Place sleeve in armscye of zip-in lining, looking into sleeve. Baste sleeve to zip-in lining and lining, keeping sleeve lining folded back. Shrink out fullness and machine stitch. Grade, or blend, seams by trimming each layer to a different width, and bring zip-in sleeve lining over seams, and hand-finish.

Lining and coat slide fasteners should be accurately aligned. The lining should zip from right to left unless otherwise is preferred. Fig. 340.

QUESTIONS

1. How do you determine the type of lining to be used?
2. Where do slide fasteners end on fully lined coats?
3. Where is the slide fastener attached to a garment?
4. What must you remember when making half-lined garments?
5. What pattern do you use for a zip-in lining?
6. How do you line a zip-in lining?
7. How is the armscye treated when sleeves are eliminated?

"The lining should zip from right to left ..."

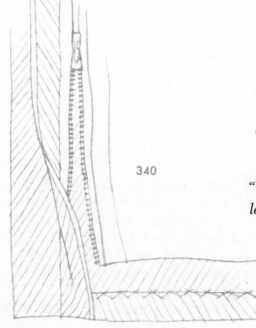

340

8. What is the procedure for putting sleeves in zip-in linings?
9. How are wristlets attached?
10. How should the lining zip in a garment?

Dresses

Interfaced Silk or Cotton Dresses

Shrink all interfacings before using. Cut the interfacing as indicated in the diagram, extending it across the shoulder to the armscye. Fig. 341. When cutting facing, extend it also to the armscye so it will conceal the interfacing.

When making bound buttonholes, baste interfacing to front and press thoroughly. Make buttonholes through interfacing. This helps to reinforce the buttonholes, Fig. 342.

Cut the seam margin from the interfacing and catch-stitch to the front, Fig. 343. When joining facing to front, stitch close to interfacing but not into it. This eliminates bulky seams.

Flat-stitch facing and front seam

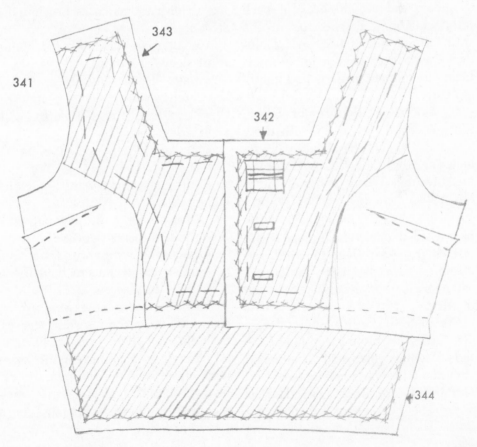

159

margins. The interfacing may be machine stitched when setting in the sleeve, or it may be overcast around the armscye after the sleeve is in. The preferred method is to overcast, or backstitch, interfacing to armscye by hand. Since the armscye is a curved seam, it is best to work with just two layers of fabric, and attach the interfacing last.

When the dress has a separate bodice piece, it should be interfaced separately, as shown, Fig. 344, page 159, and should always be lined.

Remove seam allowance across shoulders and around neck of back interfacing, and catch-stitch at the stitching line across neck and shoulder. Catch-stitch lower edge of interfacing to garment at darts and lightly at center back.

If material is lightweight fabric, the bodice may be lined with dress material. If not, the separate lining material would be attached to the dress facing. When bodice lining is eliminated, facings should always cover interfacings. Facings should be backstitched or catch-stitched to interfacings to keep them together, and anchored to a dart with as large a catch-stitch as is necessary to reach the dart.

Complete the bodice before attaching to skirt, with the exception of the slide fastener which will be attached after the garment is assembled.

If sleeves are lined, baste them as in previous instructions for coats and suits. Then crease-baste the decided length, press and trim lining to crease. Catch-stitch lining to crease of sleeve hem with large stitches. Trim hem of sleeve to 1½" or 2" (never wider) depending upon diameter of sleeve. Machine stitch close to raw edge of sleeve hem. When fabric frays easily, place two rows of small machine stitches around raw edge of hem. Catch-stitch machine stitched edge to lining, being careful not to pick up top part of sleeve.

When buttonholes are at bottom of sleeve, interface with organdy, and make buttonholes through interfacing. Finish the same as previous instructions.

An alternate method for lining short sleeves follows:

- Make sleeves and sleeve linings separately.
- Place lining inside sleeves, with right sides facing.
- Machine stitch regular seam allowance.
- Turn all seams toward lining and flat-stitch.
- Turn sleeve right side out with lining pulled inside sleeve.
- Press and baste around armscye, 2" from stitching line to hold lining and sleeve in place.

Follow previous instructions on suits and coats for inserting sleeves, with one exception—trim seams to ¼" all around instead of varying seam width from shoulder to underarm. If heavy, or bulky, fabrics are used, blend seams when trimming, for a smoother finish.

In silk dresses, the collar may be shaped any way desired in order to roll it, by quilting with fine, silk thread. Follow previous instructions on tailor's padding. If using sheer material, catch-stitch a top collar lining, minus the seam margin to top collar, then join to the padded undercollar. Trim the seam margins, turn and edge-baste.

This faced top collar prevents the padding stitches of the undercollar and interfacing from showing through. This also applies to lapels.

Padding may be done with drapery type basting, in which case the facing of top collar, or lapels, may be eliminated. Catch-stitch the interfacing to undercollar, across neck edge, minus seam allowance, Fig. 345. Using a running basting stitch, baste interfacing and undercollar together, ½″ inside catch-stitched edge of interfacing, Fig. 346. Hold the undercollar in the left hand, and fold it back over fingers. Turn interfacing back toward thumb and hold it in place. Take a small stitch in undercollar, continuing through fold of in-

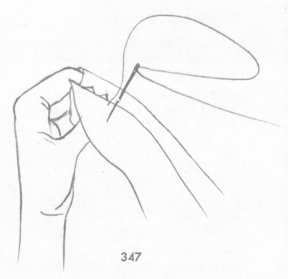

347

terfacing, picking up just a thread each time, Fig. 347. This type of drapery basting keeps the stitches between facing and interfacing invisible. The distance between stitches of drapery basting determines the firmness of collar and lapels when completed. Continue working backward and forward on collar and interfacing until completely padded with drapery basting. Shape the undercollar and attach the top collar as in previous instructions.

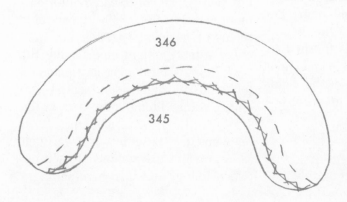

346

345

"Using a running basting stitch, baste interfacing and . . ."

161

Attaching Skirt to Dress

When lining skirts for dresses, follow instructions for lining skirts, leaving the seam open which will hold the slide fastener. The slide fastener should be placed in the garment after the bodice and skirt have been joined together.

When the skirt has been lined, and completed to slide fastener opening, attach skirt, and lining to bodice only, leaving the bodice lining free. Blend skirt and bodice seams and baste together. Complete slide fastener, keeping lining folded back and out of way. Hand-finish around the slide fastener and waist of skirt with a blind felling stitch.

Finishing Skirt Hems

Skirts may be finished as in previous instructions, or the following method may be used. Finish the skirt hem as if it were unlined by catch-stitching lightly to garment. *Never use seam tape.* Baste the lining down, folded over skirt hem, as in a coat lining, approximately ½″ shorter than the finished hem. Keep lining basting near raw edge of garment hem. Do not let lining seam margin extend more than ½″ where it is finished to outer hem, or it will wrinkle and leave a crumpled finish around the hem. This type of hem is very good for active people.

Lining a Sheath Dress

Baste and fit dress accurately before lining. Top lining should be cut the same as top garment. Close shoulder seams of dress and lining separately. Place right sides of dress and lining together, and machine stitch around neck. Turn all seam margins toward lining and flat-stitch from the right side. Stay-baste shoulder seam of lining and dress together as in previous instructions. When using a facing around the neck, catch-stitch lining to neck of dress, minus seam allowance. Baste and machine stitch facing and garment around neck. Flat-stitch facing and garment together, and catch-stitch lower edge of facing to lining, Fig. 348.

Before closing the side seams of a garment, baste front sections of lining and garment together. Keep bastings about 2″ from the side seams. Baste down center front and through center of darts to hold lining in place. Check to be sure there are no bubbles in lining or garment sections. Pinch darts between thumb and forefinger, baste, machine stitch, cut, and press open. Trim away excess dart lining and catch-stitch garment dart to lining, being sure *not* to catch outer garment fabric, Fig. 349. Baste side seams of garment together and machine stitch *garment only.* Bring the back lining section over and place on top of front, right sides facing. Machine stitch lining side seams the same width as garment seams. Press open and stay-baste to top of garment as in previous instructions. Reach between linings and turn garment right

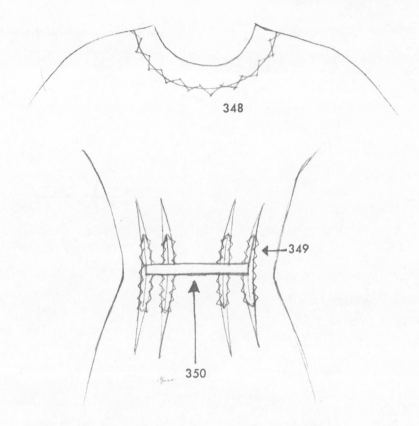

348

349

350

side out. It is easier to complete lining and stay-baste to garment before attaching the facing. If the garment has a back or side slide fastener, finish as a placket and slip-stitch lining to slide fastener tape. Finish sleeves and hem as in previous instructions. A stay, made of ribbon tape, may be tacked at darts and seams at waistline, either all around and hooked together at garment closure, or across garment front. This keeps the waistline of a sheath in place. Fig. 350.

QUESTIONS

1. How are interfacings, and facings, cut for dresses?

2. Why is interfacing catch-stitched to front?

3. How may a facing be finished after it has been machine stitched to a garment?

4. Describe the sewing in of sleeves when interfaced.

5. Give three methods of finishing dress bodices.

6. Should the bodice be completed before attaching to the skirt?

7. How are collars and lapels of dresses most commonly padded?

8. How are skirts prepared for attaching to bodice of dress?

9. How do you finish the seam when attaching the bodice lining to a skirt?

163

10. How do dress hems differ from skirt hems?
11. What section of a dress and lining are closed first?
12. How is the lining temporarily attached to front of garment?
13. Are lining darts and dress darts sewn together?
14. How are side seams of lining and dress attached?
15. How are lining and dress completed?

"Complete darts a n d pockets in front sections. Finish w i t h extended padding . . ."

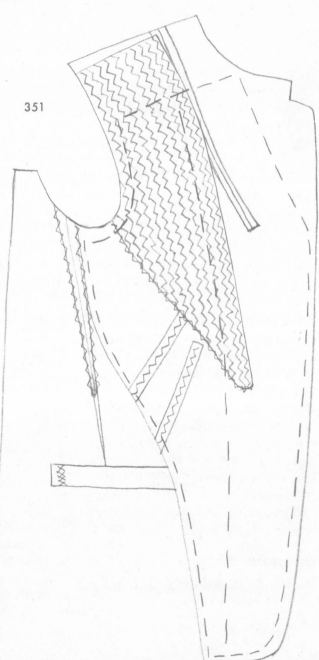

351

5. Men's Tailoring

Casual or Suit Coats

Construct garment sections according to previous instructions. Cut, tailor tack, baste, and try on.

After fitting and determining lapel, or rever, and collar break line, pocket placements and general fitting, construction may begin. Complete darts and pockets in front sections. Finish with extended padding on interfacing and attach to front sections, Fig. 351, page 164.

Baste bridle strap to break line of revers, through foundation and front, easing a little fullness of garment onto the tape. Do not quilt beyond the roll line or rever crease, on men's clothing.

The rever may be quilted to the tape, or bridle strap, or the tape may be catch-stitched on both edges after the revers are padded. The bridle strap should be underneath the lapel crease.

After pad-stitching lapels, dampen, press and lay fronts together and pin, to check accuracy. Trim ½" away on interfacing, from collar notch, down fronts to end of facing. Complete tape as in previous instructions, by whipping to interfacing. Baste facing on to front section with very little ease around padded area. Press and machine stitch through outer edge of tape, front, and front facing, in one operation. Never blend facing seam margin wider than ¼", and the front seam a fraction less.

Continue, using previous instructions for edge basting and diagonal basting around fronts. Attach front linings to facings at this point. If lining pocket extends into front facing, attach facing and lining together before making the pocket. If not, the pocket may be put into lining before attaching. Continue finishing lining to fronts as in previous instructions. When making jackets that receive hard wear, make the pockets out of silesia or a similar fabric. Complete the vent in the back section of garment before attaching to side seams.

Finishing Vents

Whenever possible, in cutting out a garment, leave vent on fold of fabric and cut on folded line just before finishing. This prevents fraying. Machine stitch back seam to vent opening, clip and press open. Press vent toward the left back section and catch-stitch together on right side of garment to keep in place. Keep stitches exactly in crease of vent, Fig. 352, page 166.

Catch-stitch a piece of stay-tape on the underneath portion of vent near

352

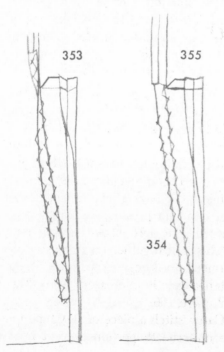

353

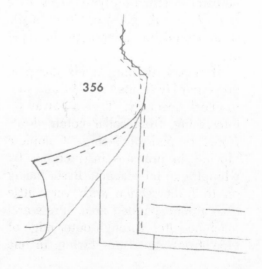

354

355

356

to hem crease. This diagonal placement of tape keeps stitches invisible from the right side of garment. Catch-stitch tape under seam allowance— at clipped place, Fig. 353, skipping approximately 2″ and then catch-stitching again down one side of the tape and back up the other, Fig. 354. Whether the coats are fully lined or half-lined, the vents are treated in the same manner.

Machine stitch the vent pieces together across the top, but not into the garment, Fig. 355.

Fully Lined Jackets

After the lining is inserted, baste up each side of the vent and across the top to hold the lining and back together. A freedom pleat is necessary when coats have vents.

Trim 1″ from the edge of the lining on the lap part of vent, allowing for seam. Clip into lining diagonally. Baste the lining to the opposite side

the crease, extending beyond clipped portion of seam.

On top section of vent, baste and press seam margin and slip a piece of stay-tape under this seam. Stay-baste or catch-stitch tape diagonally, down

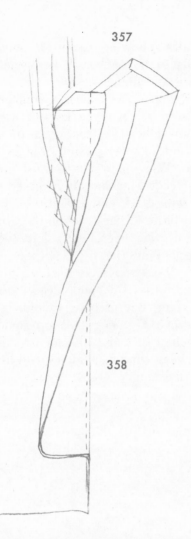

357

358

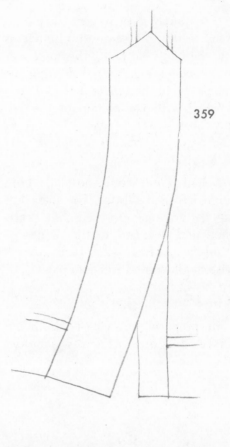

359

of vent, tucking the top of lining under where it is clipped.

Fell the lining to vent by hand with a blind finishing stitch, and around the corner at hemline for about 1″, in the same manner as garment fronts are finished, Fig. 356.

Jackets with Partially Lined Backs

When using a vent facing for un-lined or partially lined jackets, machine stitch to right back section of vent, Fig. 357, and flat stitch, Fig. 358. Be sure vent facing extends above clipped section of seam.

Finish underneath fold of vent, with a felling stitch. Using small stitches, alternate by stitching into the outer garment section and then into the seam allowance. When picking up stitches in outer garment, be sure to pick up a thread from underneath section of fabric. This stitch cannot be taut or it will be visible from right side of garment.

167

Completely attach vent facing to coat, using this same stitch. Hems may be hand-finished either under or over facings, Fig. 359. If desired, the vent may be basted and then hand-finished with completion of the lining. See drawing, page 167.

Half-back Linings

A half lining would normally be a single layer of fabric. The back lining pattern may be used, but shortened and hemmed to the length of wing-backs, Fig. 360. It is always wise to allow for a freedom pleat.

Wing-back Linings

In preparing a wing-back lining, baste diagonally across shoulder blades, allowing room for shoulder pads to be anchored, between garment and lining.

If you do not have a commercial pattern for wing-backs, cut as diagram indicates, keeping them wide enough to cover shoulder blades, Fig. 361. Wing-back linings must always be faced. Machine stitch curved edge of wing-back and flat stitch. Press, and baste to back section of garment on curved edge, with left section overlapping the right at neck, Fig. 362. Fold top section of wing-back out of the way, and baste close to stitching line of back shoulders and armscye, Fig. 363. This top section is left free so that pads can be slipped between wing-back facing and lining, for finishing.

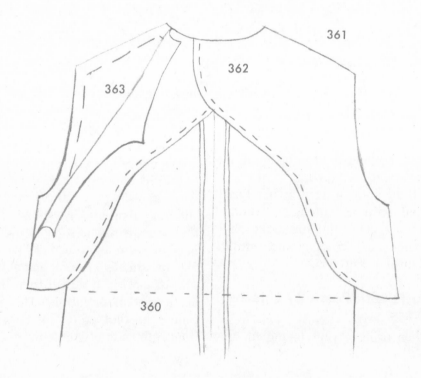

361

362

363

360

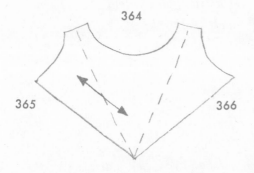

364

365 366

Completing Lined Jackets

Sweat shields may be made from single layers of lining fabric, or interlined with silesia, outing flannel, or any absorbent fabric. Cut sweat shields as shown in Fig. 364. Bring Figs. 365 and 366 together and close with an underarm dart seam in one operation. Fold at fold lines and press, forming a triangular shield, Fig. 367, page 170.

Join side sections of garment together and press seams open. Turn under front lining so the crease will meet the stitching line, and baste for later hand-finishing, Fig. 368. The front lining always overlaps the wing-back at side seam. See page 170.

Close shoulder seams, catching under section of wing-back in the same stitching, when using this type of lining. It is always necessary to ease back section of shoulder to front sections. Machine stitch and press seams open.

Men's collars are most always attached completely by hand, but any one of the previous instructions on collar-making may be used. When using wool felt undercollar fabric, the raw edge is felled to the garment across the neck edge—never turned under. The tape along the break line extends up into the collar and is catch-stitched to the collar linen. When the collar is completed, baste in sleeves, and fit pads for final finishing of linings. Fit carefully with pads to see if the sleeves drape correctly from the shoulders. Shrink out fullness and machine stitch as in previous instructions. In men's tailoring, clip coat seam allowance at two points about 3″ on either side of shoulder seam in order to press sleeve and garment seam open. This should be done before the final fitting and insertion of shoulder pads. Press carefully after each operation.

Place curved section of pad approximately 3″ from shoulder seam into front of garment, Fig. 369. The elongated section of pad should extend into the back until the tip meets the stitching line of sleeve and garment at armscye, Fig. 370. Baste pads firmly in place from right side for try-ons, and finishing later. When using a half-lining of wing-back style, the pads fit between the wing-back sections. Catch-stitch curved edge of pad to facing of wing-back lining. When using a single half-back lining, the pads will not be catch-stitched to the back lining, or the garment, on the curved section of pad. In this style, only the front is catch-stitched. Trim pads and seam allowance the length of the pad from ⅜″ at tips to

169

*"Fold at fold lines and press, forming a triangular shield. . . . Turn
under front lining so the crease will meet . . ."*

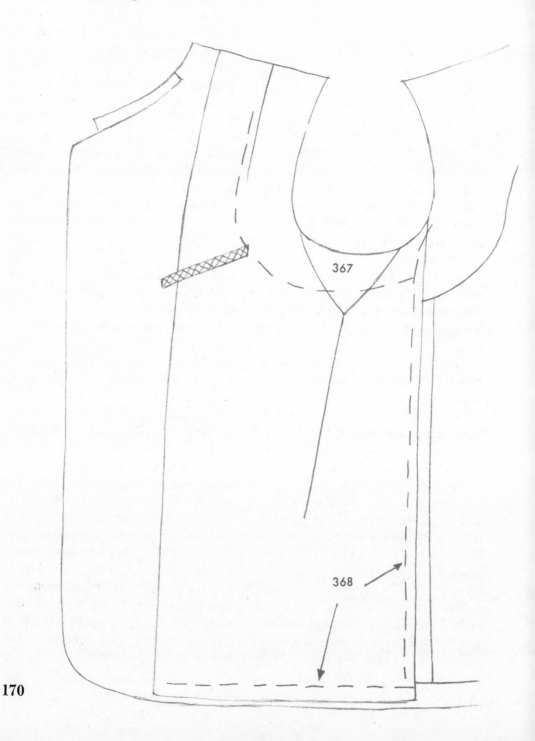

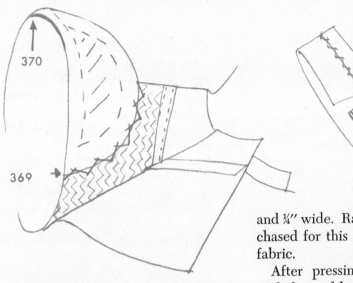

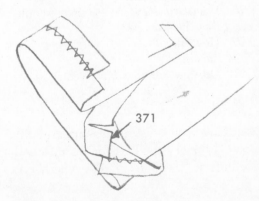

½″ at shoulder seam. Overcast or stay-stitch pad lightly to seam allowance of sleeve and garment. Stab-stitching leaves a little more fluff in the pad if more padding is desired. (See Hand-Tailoring Stitches, pages 29 and 30.)

In set-in sleeves, follow previous instructions for attaching the sleeve welt.

Permanently baste lining and garment together as in previous instructions for final finishing.

If desired, a hanger may be sewn across the back of neck at the base of collar. It should be about 2″ long and ¼″ wide. Rayon tape may be purchased for this purpose, or use lining fabric.

After pressing the garment, buttonholes and buttons may be worked. When having a garment professionally pressed, complete with the exception of buttons and buttonholes.

Sleeve Vents

Close seams to sleeve opening for vent. Clip seam margin to stitching line on the under sleeve section.

Turn sleeve to the right side, place on a sleeve board and press vent flat as though it were a pleat, using press cloth. Catch-stitch vent to crease of hem.

Baste interfacing of wigan to bottom of sleeve all the way to the crease of vent. Measure sleeve length and crease-baste the bottom.

Press sleeve on wrong side with vertical strokes. This shrinks fullness from the sleeve hem.

Cut square section inside of vent fold, below crease of hem, Fig. 371. Fold the remainder of hem diagonally across the hem and finish by hand, Fig. 372.

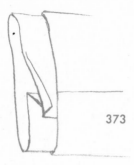

373

Note: Vents should lay flat when finished. Tuck the raw edges of hem in about ¼″ on the opposite side, and finish by hand.

Catch-stitch extended wigan interfacing of hem *only* to sleeve seam margin on underarm and overarm seams.

Do not make vents in sleeve lining. Stitch seam straight and finish about 1¼″ shorter than the sleeve, Fig. 373. Work false buttonholes and place buttons on the outside. Make bound buttonholes, if putting vents in ladies' garments.

QUESTIONS

1. After the coat is fitted, how is break line of rever and collar determined?
2. How do men's interfacings differ from ladies'?
3. What is the function of the bridle strap?
4. Where does the pad stitching start on a rever?
5. Why are the facings treated differently when linings are attached?
6. When do you finish the vent in the back seam?
7. Why is it best to cut a vent on the fold line?
8. How is a vent pressed? Where is it catch-stitched?
9. How do you reinforce vents?
10. What is necessary in fully lined coats with vents?
11. How are vents in fully lined garments finished?
12. How are vents finished in partially lined jackets?
13. How may coat hems be finished?
14. How long should a half-back lining be?
15. How can a wing-back lining be cut without a pattern?
16. Why are wing-back linings double?
17. What material is used to make sweat shields? Where are they placed?
18. How do you finish the side seam of a front lining, in half-back or wing-back lining?
19. How are men's collars most often finished?
20. How do seams of sleeves and armscyes differ?
21. What type of shoulder pad is used for men's garments? How is it placed?
22. Do you finish men's shoulder pads the same as ladies'?
23. Where do you sew collar hangers?
24. When do you make buttonholes and sew on buttons?
25. What are sleeve vents? How should they be pressed?
26. How should hems, with vents, be finished?
27. Do sleeve linings have vents?

Vests or Waist Coats

This article of men's apparel fits snugly over the chest for warmth and comfort. Fashion decrees whether it is made of matching suit material, or a contrasting fabric (small or large check, subtle or bold plaid, knitted fabric, etc.). It is usually lined with silesia or sateen and interlined with wigan, and the outer back is suit lining fabric.

A vest requires careful measuring, cutting, and fitting and should be constructed as carefully as a suit coat. The neck seam should barely cover the shirt collar seam. Buttons should be about 2″ apart and about ⅝″ from the edge of the vest front, and there are six, unless the person is very short-waisted. The top button should be about 2½″ below the armpit, and the lower one at the waist. In length, the vest should cover the trouser belt. Measure from center back of prominent neck bone, around to center of chest about 2½″ below armpit, and to 1½″ below the waist.

Baste wigan interlining to vest fronts.

Pockets are placed 4″ from center front and 4″ above the waist. The upper pocket is 4″ wide and 2½″ from underarm; the lower pocket is 4½″ wide and both should slant upward ¾″. Pocket depth should finish at about 5″. Make pockets following lapel or breast pocket instructions.

After the pockets are completed, trim wigan away at center front, and tape, as in coat front instructions, holding the tape slightly taut from 2″ below the shoulder to the top button. This causes the garment to lay close to the chest. The facing can now be attached down the front and across the bottom. When sewing lining to the front, keep lining fuller than outer garment. Pull front lining around front at armscye and machine stitch from shoulder to side seam. Turn right side out and press. Join back and back lining in center, and press seams open.

Lay back lining on table right side up, and place front side seams on back with linings facing each other. Place vest back on top lining back with fronts in between and baste and machine stitch across shoulder, down armscye, side seams, and across the bottom. Reach inside neck and turn right side out. Baste and stitch the neck together at center back. Attach back of vest across back to neck band, and press open. Press facing to lay flat and fell lining on inside of vest at the neck.

For final finishing, stitch along edge of vest front across the bottom and around the neck, and cut and work buttonholes. The fronts should lap approximately 1″.

QUESTIONS

1. How are vests fitted? What is the proper length?
2. Where should the top button of a vest be placed?
3. What style pocket is used, and where are they placed?
4. How are the fronts of waist coats, or vests, finished?
5. Explain the procedure in joining the back and front of a vest.

Men's trousers must be fitted carefully, but they are easier to construct than coats.

• Establish the individual preference by measuring the inseam of well-fitting trousers from crotch to cuff turn.

• Measure outseam, including waistband.

• Measure hips at fullest point.

• Measure waist and bottom of trouser.

• Compare these measurements to pattern sections and adjust pattern accordingly.

When working from measurements alone, measure to the floor with the individual barefooted, and add 5″ for cuff finishing. If no cuff is used, allow 2″ for a hem.

The width of the bottom of the trouser leg should be determined by the shoe size. For a size 8 shoe, 19″ would be the correct circumference. (With trousers lying on a flat surface, the measurement would be 9½″.) Increase this figure by ½″ for each shoe size. Larger trouser bottoms minimize shoe size. If a tapered trouser style is desired, taper gradually from knee to cuff.

Approximately 2″ should be added to the thigh measurement, and ½″ to the waist measurement for ease.

When buttocks are full and high, Fig. 374, add more to the back and raise the waist slightly, Fig. 375. Sometimes this type of figure requires a shorter front. If trousers have bias wrinkles in front, fold waist the needed amount and trim, until they fit smoothly over the abdomen. When the reverse is true, and wrinkles appear over the seat, Fig. 376, increase the front, if necessary, and decrease the center back seam, Fig. 377.

If the abdomen is large, an unpressed dart, or pleat will make the

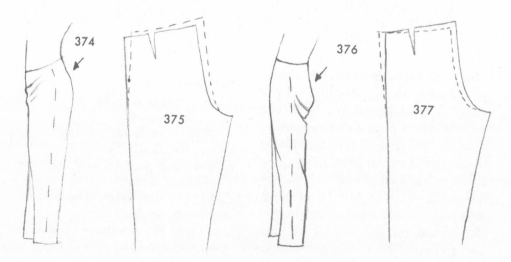

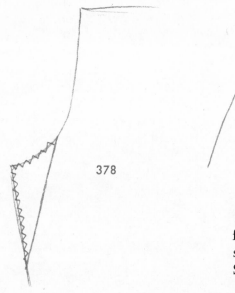

RIGHT SIDE

379

378

trousers more attractive and comfortable. To make this pleat from a plain pattern, slash pattern from waist to below knee, or to ⅛″ from hem, whichever amount is needed, and spread apart to create a pleat.

If there is a weight problem, add an extra amount on the seat seam and inside the back leg seam, starting at crotch and tapering to nothing at the knee.

Back pockets are placed about 4½″ or 5″ below, and parallel to the waist, and 2″ from the outside seam. The width of the pocket is determined by the size of the individual—from 5″ to 6″. This pocket can be made with a flap and single or double welt, or a plain single welt. Back pockets should finish 7″ deep.

Cut and serge raw seams of trousers. Baste bias piece of wigan in

front crotch, Fig. 378. Baste trouser sections together and try on for fit. Sew back darts and make hip pockets.

Baste pocket piece on inside of trousers, covering pocket mouthline. Cut welt piece approximately 3″ x 6″ or 7″, depending on length of mouthline, and baste with right sides facing. The welt piece should extend 1″ above, 2″ below and ½″ on each end of mouthline. Machine stitch welt piece to trousers ⅛″ above and below, and across each end of mouthline, catching underneath the pocket sections which acts as a pocket interfacing, Fig. 379. Turn to wrong side and cut from center to ⅛″ from ends, and diagonally to each corner, Fig. 380. Turn trousers to the right side, pull welt piece through mouthline, equally divide welts, and baste. Catch-stitch welts together, baste lower edge of welt to pocket piece on inside, and press. Top stitch trousers along lower edge of pocket welt, Fig. 381. Zigzag lower edge of welt piece to pocket piece. If fabric is light in

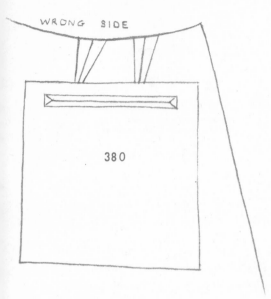

WRONG SIDE

380

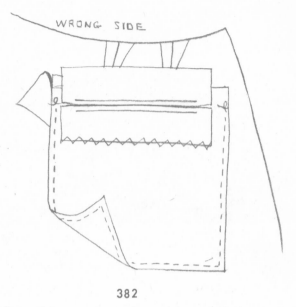

WRONG SIDE

382

weight, this may be crease-stitched. Place top pocket piece on top of under pocket and notch both on each side, approximately ½″ above welt. Flip underpocket up toward waistband, and place top pocket over it with right sides facing, matching notches. Stitch a ⅛″ seam from notch to notch. Turn pocket to right side and place second row of stitching completely around pocket, forming a French seam, Fig. 382. Turn back to right side of trousers and top stitch across ends and along upper edge of

pocket welt. This stitching is shown on the wrong side in Fig. 383.

Place side pocket facing on trouser front with right sides facing, and sew between notches, catching pocket. Clip to stitching line and press seam

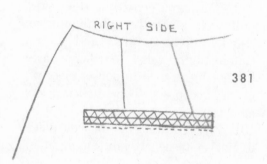

RIGHT SIDE

381

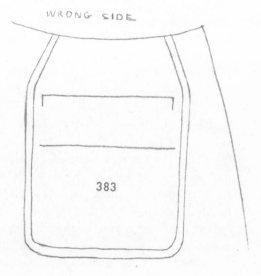

WRONG SIDE

383

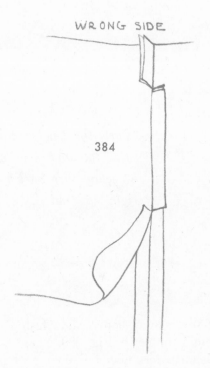

WRONG SIDE

384

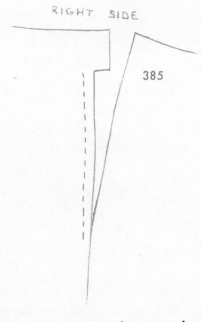

RIGHT SIDE

385

385

open, Fig. 384. Turn, edge baste and stitch facing to pocket on the inside. Top stitch pocket welt between notches, Fig. 385. Attach opposite pocket facing, Fig. 386. Turn the pocket inside out and sew a ⅛″ seam; turn back to right side and stitch a French seam, Fig. 387. Diagonally baste along pocket welt to keep it in place. See page 178.

The right front fly section should be finished approximately 4″ from center crotch seam. Baste slide fastener ⅛″ inside stitching line which joins the front trouser legs, and stitch. Finish fly section at curved seam. Machine stitch fly section to trouser front by stitching just outside previous slide fastener stitching. Baste fly-facing to trouser front to keep in

place. Join trouser legs together at side seams, keeping the pocket folded out of the way, and press seams open, Fig. 388. Tuck pocket edge under at side seam and hand-finish, or machine stitch.

Most waistbands are finished 1½″ wide and 1½″ longer than each trouser half. Place waistband on trouser half with right sides facing. Machine stitch and press band and trouser seams open. Commercially prepared waistband facings may be purchased at tailor supply houses, or they may be made from a strip of silesia, 3½″ wide and as long as the trouser band, cut on the bias, and interfaced with crinoline or some permanent stiffening fabric. Attach facing to the upper edge of band, turn all seams toward facing, slip stiffening underneath facing and catch with flat or zigzag

177

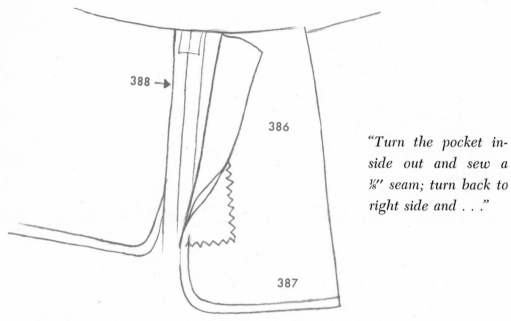

388 →

386

387

"Turn the pocket inside out and sew a ⅛" seam; turn back to right side and . . ."

stitch. If using a hook and eye closure on the fly facing, this must be put in before waistband is closed permanently. When using button and buttonhole, they may be done after trousers have been completed. If slide fastener is too long, cut off extension

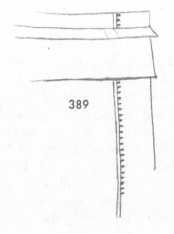

389

and sew slowly across slide fastener through the teeth, Fig. 389.

Belt carriers may be sewn on top after the trousers are completed, or they may be sewn in with the waistband. This is a stronger method.

The watch, or change pocket, is placed approximately 1½" from the side seam on the right side of trousers. Do not rip waistband from trousers at this point, but mark where pocket mouthline should be, about 2¼" wide when finished. Cut pocket from silesia about 7" by 3¼". Attach facing of trouser fabric, about 1" by 3¼", at one edge of pocket. Sew faced edge of pocket to waistband seam margin, and flat-stitch. Attach opposite end of silesia to trouser seam margin. Close sides of pocket, rounding corners. This pocket may remain sewn shut until waistband is completed.

Turn under lower edge of waistband facing, deeply enough to catch it when top stitching at waistline. Fold fly-facing back over right side of waistband and stitch around corner. Turn and press. Top stitch from base of slide fastener to upper edge of waistband, and back to waistline, proceeding around band at waistline. Stitch on trouser at waistline until watch pocket is reached. At this point, cross over to band side of waistline and stitch there to end of watch pocket. Then, cross back over to trousers and continue around waistline to approximately 1½″ from center back. Match bobbin thread to facing and pocket fabric, and top thread to trouser fabric.

Baste fly interfacing on the wrong side of left front. Place fly facing on right side with right sides facing. Stitch regular seam width along the edge. Press seam open, back together and flat-stitch. Baste along edge to hold in place. Match crotch seams of trouser legs and sew together from seams to slide fastener. Baste left side of trousers over slide fastener. Turn to inside and baste edge of fastener tape to facing only, and machine stitch. Baste facing and interfacing to trousers from right side, around outer edge. Top stitch around fly facing, using the basting as a guide line. Cut extended portion of slide fastener and tape, and stitch band to trousers on right side, being sure waist closures are in place before the band is sealed.

Press crotch seams open, and lay extended edge of right fly facing over it, turning edges under. Baste in place for later finishing.

Baste seat of trousers and try on for final fitting. Machine stitch now, or when cuffs have been completed.

Turn trousers wrong side out, with seams matched, and measure length from inseam to base. Lay ruler at bottom of trousers and mark length with chalk. Fold trouser leg back over ruler and mark opposite side of leg. Place two marks, 2″ apart and below previous mark—less, if a narrower cuff is desired. Mark the other trouser leg in same manner.

Turn trousers to right side and turn up cuff to correct trouser length. Turn down at second mark to form cuff. Fold lower edge under and crease-baste. Try on to check length, and machine stitch raw edge to inside of trouser leg.

For final finishing, the belt carriers may be top stitched at base and top of waistband with bar tacking or by stitching back and forth several times. Bar tack ends of pockets and base of slide fastener, for strength. Work buttonhole in left hip pocket, ¼″ below welt, and sew on button. Waistband button and buttonhole should be finished at this time. Hand-finish the lower extension of fly facing, or machine stitch.

QUESTIONS

1. What is the first step in making trousers?

2. How is the width of trouser bottoms determined?
3. How do you fit high buttocks?
4. Where are back pockets placed? How wide are they? How deep?
5. Give a brief summary of hip pocket construction.
6. When are side front pockets finished?
7. At what point is a slide fastener attached to the front?
8. How is a waistband completed?
9. Where is the watch pocket placed?
10. Why are the right and left legs constructed separately?
11. Why are the pockets, belt carriers, and the base of fly closure, bar tacked?

Glossary

Beeswax. A small cake of wax across which thread is pulled to give it strength and keep it from snarling.

Blending. Trimming each layer of a seam to a different width to avoid bulkiness.

Bridle strap. A strong, unstretchable strip of cotton sewn to the interfacing at crease of revers.

Bubble. A puffed area in the outer layer of a garment, which occurs when the lining, interfacing, or underneath fabrics, are too taut.

Cheese block. A half-circle of smooth hardwood, used to press curved sections of garments, such as collars, sleeve crowns, etc.

Collar drop. Part of a collar from crease to finished edge.

Collar notch. Area between the lapel, or rever, and where collar is attached to garment.

Drawing in. A term used for easing fullness in an armscye, etc., with a backstitch, before shrinking it away by pressing.

Drop. See *Collar Drop*.

Easing. Joining a fuller section to a less full section by slightly gathering the fuller piece and stitching with the gathered piece uppermost.

Felling. Hand-finishing one section to another, using neat, invisible stitches.

Felting. A pounding process, used in producing felt, which joins the serrated fibers without weaving.

Findings. Items, other than the garment and lining fabric, required to complete the garment: interfacings, buttons, shoulder pads, thread, and various forms of trimmings.

Freedom pleat. A fold p l a c e d at points in the lining of a garment where ease is necessary to assure comfort and action.

Frog fastener. A decorative closing fastener, usually a clover leaf design, made of cording. It may be hand made, but is available at notions counters and tailoring supply houses.

Gimp. A heavy thread used as a stay, to keep the openings of hand-worked buttonholes from stretching out of shape.

Grading. Changing the size of a garment pattern to a larger, or smaller, size. Also see *Blending*.

Hymo. A term tailors use to identify interfacings made of various combinations of wool, goat hair, cotton, and linen, as opposed to the synthetics.

Interfacing. Material, such as haircloth, canvas, linen, etc., used in making the foundations to which garments are molded.

Lay of material. Fabric laid out with pattern in place, preparatory to cutting.

Mouthline. The opening of a pocket, or buttonhole.

Padding stitch. A stitch used in attaching interfacing to collar and lapel, and in shaping the desired roll. Also called Tailor's Quilting.

Pounding block. A polished hardwood block used to flatten seams and finished edges.

Purl. A stitch which forms a knot, used in making hand-worked buttonholes.

Raw edge. An unfinished seam.

Revers. A lapel.

Scye. An old term for armscye, or armhole.

Serging. A special machine finish, used on raw seams of ready-made garments to restrain fraying. It resembles a single crochet stitch.

Shaping. Trimming the fronts of a garment to smooth, straight lines, the correct distance from buttonholes, before taping and attaching facing.

Sheath. A common term for fine cotton sheath lining, used to line, or back, garments.

Shirr. To draw cloth together evenly, using very small stitches, to make a decorative gathering of material.

Silesia. Strong cotton twill used for trouser pockets and waistband facings.

Sleeve welt. A strip of cotton sheet wadding sewn to the cut edge of shoulder pads and sleeves.

Stay-basting. A basting left in a garment to keep sections together.

Stay tape. A specially woven linen, or cotton, tape used to prevent stretching of fronts.

Straight grain. Parallel to selvedge of fabric.

Vent. An opening used at wrist of sleeves, hem of skirts, and back of coats.

Wigan. A strong, specially woven cotton fabric used for reinforcing pocket mouthlines, sleeves, and garment hems.

Index